FROM KOLKATA

FROM KOLKATA TO WALES

THE GROUNDBREAKING JOURNEY OF THE UK'S FIRST FEMALE ASIAN CONSULTANT

Tapati Guha Maulik

YOUCAXTON
PUBLICATIONS

Copyright © Tapati Maulik 2021

The Author asserts the moral right to
be identified as the author of this work.

ISBN 978-1-913425-89-0
Published by YouCaxton Publications 2021
YCBN: 01

All rights reserved. No part of this publication may be reproduced, stored in a retrieval system, or transmitted in any form or by any means, electronic, mechanical, photocopying, recording or otherwise, without the prior permission of the author.

This book is sold subject to the condition that it shall not, by way of trade or otherwise, be lent, resold, hired out or otherwise circulated without the author's prior consent in any form of binding or cover other than that in which it is published and without a similar condition including this condition being imposed on the subsequent purchaser.

YouCaxton Publications
www.youcaxton.co.uk

In memory of my parents.

Preface

FROM SOMEWHERE WITHIN myself I felt I should write about my journey from a junior doctor in India to becoming a Consultant Obstetrician and Gynaecologist in the United Kingdom, a journey which had many hurdles. I should have written it when I retired but instead I did a lot of travelling. When Covid 19 appeared from nowhere and with Lockdown implemented, I felt now was the time to write as I was almost housebound.

I grew up in Indian culture and travelled to United Kingdom for higher studies where the culture was different. I had to adjust and accommodate myself which took a bit of time. Amidst racism, I needed to fight in order to be climb up the ladder on the job front. Colleagues I worked with avoided me initially till I won their hearts by showing my capabilities and friendliness. They changed their attitude towards me and supported me. There were some who could not imagine coloured people working in senior posts and these were the people to look out for.

Being a woman, I had to suffer more as this used-to-be-a-man's world and they felt they were more intelligent. Thank goodness this is changing. It has been fascinating to live and work in a foreign country where I have had to be stronger and better than the local colleagues in order to climb up the ladder.

I enjoyed living in a challenging environment and felt that women were not inferior to men. Given the opportunity, women are equal to men if not better. It's the will power makes you successful so women should not give up because the hard work pays off.

Tapati Guha Maulik, FRCOG
Merthyr Tydfil

Contents

Preface vii
1. EARLY DAYS 1
2. PRE REGISTRATION REQUIREMENTS 6
3. ANAESTHESIA 10
4. LONG ASSOCIATION WITH O. & G. 14
5. SENIOR REGISTRAR ROTATION 22
6. CONSULTANT APPOINTMENT 29
7. NEW SERVICES 37
8. PUBLICATIONS 41
9. COLLEGE TUTOR & TRAINING 43
10. TRIBUNAL & LITIGATION 45
11. THE NHS 50
12. HOLIDAYS GOING WRONG 53
13. EXPENSIVE HOBBY 55
14. SERVICES PROVIDED 57
15. OBSERVATION OF NHS DECLINING 80
16. WAWAA AWARDED TROPHY 82
17. PANDEMIC 85
18. FINALLY 89

1. EARLY DAYS

I WAS BORN in India into a large Hindu family and I was the fifth child of my parents. I was fortunate to be born into this family, the descendants of an ancient line. We are descended from King Maharajah Pratapaditya, the last king of Bengal. The family was in power in the 16th Century and still there are places named after him in West Bengal and Bangladesh. Bangladesh was a part of Bengal before the British rule. After partition it was a part of Pakistan, but it broke away from Pakistan and became Bangladesh. The Maharajah was a very powerful King in the 16th century; he fought against the Moghul Imperial army and Bengal became independent. In addition to the Moghul enemy there were Portuguese and Arakanese pirates, who raided the coastal regions continuously, and he managed to fight them also. He was the last King and icon in Bengal. Pratapaditya's forefathers were also powerful. The original family tree written by my great grandfather is still with us and it goes back to the 10th Century.

My father was an engineer and worked as a Chief Superintendent of the steel plant of an Iron and Steel Company which was partner with a British Company. He met the Queen Elizabeth II when she visited the steel plant in her younger days. He had all his postgraduate degrees from UK and America. He was also trained as glass technologist and a freedom fighter in his younger days. My parents married young and this was an arranged marriage. My mother was thirteen years of age only and this used to be the norm those days. Her father was a well-known doctor and was also from a distinguished family. Although she did not have much education, she was knowledgeable. Despite having a big family, she managed to do a lot of charity work including delivering babies in the district with an American midwife. The trend in the 19th Century was for young girls to get married and their education was not a priority. I had three brothers and three sisters. They were all highly qualified and in different professions. As I write I only have a brother and a sister alive as the rest have left us. My brother is an ex-pilot for Air India, having been in the Indian Airforce before; my sister is a retired nurse who qualified in the UK but gave up work after she had children.

I am the only one who never married. My plan was to complete my post-graduate qualification before settling down. I had good friends and I was never keen on anybody. My responsibility towards my family increased when I lost my youngest brother to deadly cancer as he had left two beautiful children and a young wife. From the death bed, he requested me to look after them. Thus I stayed single as I found marriage would make it difficult for me to carry on with my career and be responsible for the wider family. I preferred to continue my life as such but kept my social life simple and uncomplicated. From the clinics I used to meet a lot of women who had disastrous family lives which may have been one of the factors that prevented me for marrying. I do not regret being alone and perhaps it has helped me in achieving the goal which I wanted.

I studied in a local school like my other brothers and sisters. As I grew up in a big family, we were friendly and cared for each other, not having to look for friends. Our parents were keen for us to do well in studies and in sports. Father was rather strict regarding our upbringing and maintained discipline. My mother was friendly with an American Lady, a trained midwife, and the wife of the managing director of the Iron and Steel Company where my father worked. This American lady used to help out in home births in the nearby villages and my mother used to assist her. My mother did this charity work while we were in school. I was fascinated by their work as I used to hear the experience they gathered when they helped the women during their deliveries. There was no National

Mrs Kamala Guha Maulik- inspiration- my mother.

Mr Sushil C Guha Maulik- my mentor- my father.

Health Service; it was a third-world country lacking in facilities and the poor people suffered due to financial difficulties.

As a child I saw poor people suffering when they were ill. They could not have proper treatment and the mortality was very high amongst this group. This made me feel that I should take up medicine, although no one in the immediate family was a doctor. My aim was to become a good doctor and help these people as much as I could. I passed Senior Cambridge from a convent school followed by Intermediate Science and obtained high grades. I was then selected in medical college to study medicine, admitted to R G Kar Medical College, under Calcutta University, in 1960 and qualified in 1965.

My plan was to come to the United Kingdom for post-graduate studies so I never worked in India and came straight to the UK as a trainee, although I was not sure at that stage what I was going to specialise in. My second sister was already in UK, so I knew I had a place to visit. I needed to do a pre-registration job and applied for the house physician's post in the Royal Gwent Hospital in General Medicine, twelve miles from my sister.

I got the job.

I arrived in the United Kingdom on 29 July 1966 from Kolkata and stayed with my sister for a day before I moved to the Gwent hospital. I had a room in the doctor's quarters with free meals, laundry and free accommodation and the salary was £750 per year as a preregistration doctor in general medicine.

I was getting £32 per month. It seems so little compared to a doctor's salary nowadays, but the price of food and clothing were much less. For five years I could not visit my parents in India because I did not have enough money. I got used to the bland diet of the British people; I used to have meals in the hospital cafeteria as I could not cook.

My first impression of the country was exceptionally good. People were very polite, well dressed and disciplined. Ladies wore skirts and hats rather than trousers. I did not see any obese people. They seemed to be very helpful and friendly. There were not many Asians at the time and the ones who had come were mainly doctors. There were no Indian restaurants and Asian shops in town. A good thing I got used to the food in the hospital.

I remember we were woken up in the morning by domestic staff with a cup of tea. This was a really civilised way of treating junior doctors and I loved it. This service continued for some time but gradually stopped. It was the best service I ever had in the NHS. Nowadays, one cannot dream of having any of those perks. The culture was different and I was careful and tried to acquire it slowly. The language was not a problem as I had studied in an English medium at school although I had to be careful about the dialect.

2. PRE REGISTRATION REQUIREMENTS

WHEN I JOINED Royal Gwent Hospital as a House Physician my colleague was a Chinese doctor. I was on call every other night, looking after the patients of two consultants and the emergency admissions. I was working alternate weekends as well, so the workload was very heavy. I was welcomed by the medical and nursing staff when I joined and I found them very friendly and helpful, especially because I had just come from India. The two consultants were helpful and guided me in getting used to British medicine.

I had very little time for myself as the night on call was busy. Often I was too tired to visit my sister twelve miles away and anyway I did not have a car. I learnt a lot in general medicine but I encountered problems as well. My first clinic was difficult as I had difficulty in understanding the Welsh accent. The nursing staff in the clinic helped me. I gathered some of the patients were biased and were refusing treatment from overseas doctors.

A patient was admitted as an emergency with a history of acute respiratory bronchospasm. She needed urgent treatment to relieve the spasm so that she could breathe normally. As soon as she saw me, she refused treatment from me because I was coloured. The consultant on call was informed and he advised that the patient could go home if she refused treatment from me. Unfortunately, the patient's condition deteriorated as the time was going on and I had to call the ENT doctor on call as the patient needed tracheostomy to breathe. This patient survived but did not realise how serious her condition was. The ENT doctor was from the

Indian subcontinent also. The ignorant patient survived the ordeal because of the two coloured doctors!

Making international telephone calls were difficult. In order to ring my parents, I had to book the calls in advance. The call had to go through the switchboard of the hospital. With the advancement in technology what a difference it has made now a days. Perhaps this achievement may be the cause of all the terrorism which is taking place. Things were safe, peaceful and less problematic in those days. From the wired telephone, slowly it became cordless then came mobile phones. Fax machines were invented and important data or patients' notes could be faxed through to other hospitals which was very helpful for the management of patients. Finally, we now see computers in every hospital room and in GP practises. This has been a major development in recent times Looking back, I wonder how we managed without all these facilities.

I was quite slim and small when I came to the UK and I found the patients comparatively bulky, especially the men. Trying to do neurological examinations like knee-and-ankle jerks were rather difficult due to the weight of the legs that I had to lift to do the examination. I enjoyed the clinical work despite being busy. Most of the work was done by the doctors; in those days there were no phlebotomists neither there were ECG technicians; we had to do these ourselves. Sometimes there was a shortage of porters and we had to lift the patients as well. Nobody grumbled; everyone quietly did their work. Things have all changed now so NHS workers have time for themselves, but we were more experienced than the doctors of today.

I started the job in the month of August when everything was running smoothly and I was guided by my seniors. During the winter months, the wards were full of elderly patients. There were many hypothermic patients who were coming from homes with little heating in the houses. These patients were difficult to treat. Once I misdiagnosed a patient as dead when he was hypothermic then, few seconds later, his hand moved. I was very concerned about the diagnosis and after that I was very careful and carried out all the parameters before declaring such a diagnosis.

As a house physician, I was working daily 9am to 5pm Monday to Friday with alternate nights on call. No replacements were available when the colleague was on leave or off sick, and then I had to be on call continuously. We were being exploited as there were nobody to speak for the junior doctors. On the plus side, the training was tremendous and I had very good experience in a short period. Somehow, I did not mind this training as I was learning a lot and I enjoyed the experience I was getting. I do not think any doctors nowadays would like to work like us; they seem to be of different breed and would not put up with unearthly hours of work – and I do not blame them.

After six months of medicine, I had to do six months of general surgery to complete my pre-registration training. I had the house surgeon's post in Llanelli General Hospital. This was a small hospital and I came across a lot of Welsh-speaking persons in the clinic. They were generally senior citizens who did not want to speak in English. So I managed to learn some Welsh words which helped me in the clinic, and the nurses were there to help as well. Although the unit was small, a lot of surgical procedures were carried out. I had the chance of doing small procedures like appendectomy etc. under the guidance of the registrar and the consultant. At times I had to cover the Accident and Emergency Unit, which was a part of the training. This part of the job was rather busy as emergency cases were brought in where there were skeleton staffs on duty, and history from the patient was not always available in acute cases. I lost a patient in Casualty in a matter of minutes. He complained of pain in the arms and within minutes had a cardiac arrest and died in front of me. This patient was only forty-five years old. Resuscitation was done by the whole cardiac team and me but he did not respond. This upset me very much. Nowadays, a lot of improvement has taken place and sophisticated resuscitation machines and more drugs are available including dedicated cardiac teams. Paramedics are now also trained to carry out cardiac resuscitation at the house before transferring patients to the hospital.

3. ANAESTHESIA

AFTER COMPLETING THE house jobs, I took up anaesthesia in Morriston Hospital in Swansea. This was also a busy job and involved being on duty on alternate nights.

Anaesthesia was remarkably interesting. I met surgeons from different specialities; they changed their attitude as soon as they started operating because patient's life was in their hands and they did not want anything to go wrong. I liked the job as I could observe different kinds of operations which gave me a tremendous amount of experience. The cardio-thoracic surgeon was an excellent man but was colour blind. It was good to see him operating and being colour-blind did not make him a dangerous surgeon although I don't know how he managed to do surgery being colour blind. I worked under quite a few anaesthetic consultants. For two months I was under supervision before I was allowed to anaesthetise patients on my own. Once I started on my own, I enjoyed my work and began to feel like an independent doctor. During this period, I started learning more Welsh words because I found that, after an operation was over, in order to wake up the patients, the patients responded more quickly if they heard their own language being spoken. I learnt quite a bit of Welsh including swear words – I felt, if anyone used abusive words in Welsh I would understand. I worked in that department for twelve months and I was offered a registrar's post. I turned it down as I wanted to specialise in O & G! Looking back, I feel I should have continued in this line as it was easy and not so demanding.

Morriston hospital was a friendly hospital. The resident doctors were marvellous. We helped each other out. At the time Indian food was hardly available. I did not know how to cook so I had to depend on others and I became their dish-washer and helped in the kitchen. The canteen produced British food for the patients, doctors and nurses. Occasionally Asian doctors got together and cooked curries and I used to join in with them. As I was the most junior doctor, senior doctors took advantage, making me do all the difficult jobs like cleaning all the utensils and tiding up the kitchen.

Swansea is a beautiful city and is the second largest in Wales. It has a lot of beautiful beaches. Often I used to go to the beach to relax. The main shopping complex was right in the heart of the city with various big shops around. I had a second-hand Morris Minor car that I used for driving around the city. Petrol price was cheap compared to what it is now. As the duty hours were so long, going out was infrequent but I still managed to get around. I was driving with my Indian license and managed to get the British license after second attempt as I failed the first time for driving above the speed limit.

I remember when I wanted to buy the car, I went to the bank asking for a loan for £300. The bank refused and told me that I was a foreigner who might run away with the money and my salary was too poor! I felt humiliated and told them that I did not trust their bank and I closed my account.

We three friends decided to tour the continent in the Morris Minor. We were travelling for ten days and could take £50 per person. No booking was done as accommodation was readily available. We managed the whole trip on £150 only.

We had a good time and the money we were carrying was sufficient. The problem we faced was with the language as none of us could talk any European language except English but the Europeans did not want to talk in English. They seemed to detest British people. Another problem I had was to drive on the right side of the road which I was not used to. In Frankfurt, Germany, by mistake I drove in the wrong lane in the city centre and I could see cars on four lanes were coming towards me. As I did not know what to do at the time, I put my head lights on and put up both of my hands to say 'I'm sorry'. Luckily all the cars in the four lanes stopped and allowed me to make a U turn. I thought that they were very civilised – perhaps my British number plate helped me to get away. In Switzerland I had great difficulty on the hairpin bends as the car was not powerful enough to go up them. I was helped by another driver. Now they have made tunnels so driving has become easier.

In Germany one of the tyres developed a bump on the inner side, so I took the car to a garage and the verdict by the mechanic was, 'caput on the tyre'. There was no need to do anything at the time but I must change the tyre after returning home. I understood what he meant because the word 'caput' was used in obstetrics for a swelling on the head of a new-born baby which disappears within a couple of days. The trip overall was good and we thoroughly enjoyed ourselves.

When I returned I decided to have a new car so that I could travel around Britain. I went to Citron garage to have a test-drive on a car that I fancied. The salesman asked me whether I could afford to buy it before showing me the car otherwise it would be a waste of time! I knew the price of the car and I could afford it so I walked away from that garage adamant that I would buy the same model from a different garage. I went to Cardiff and I bought a similar model and got a good discount on it. This showed that not all the people were prejudiced. The Cardiff salesman was a good businessman; he did not worry about ethnicity, he took an interest in the business. I managed to drive to the local garage to show them that they had lost a genuine customer. Since then I have changed my cars every two years and finally, when I became a consultant, I kept two cars all the time till I retired, one for the hospital and the other one for social visits. I don't know why I became very keen on cars but perhaps I liked driving.

I enjoyed my twelve months working in anaesthesia and during this period I appeared for my Diploma examination. I had done very well in the written examination but I failed in viva.

The question that the examiners asked me was: 'how would I diagnose arrhythmias of heart during induction of anaesthesia?' My answer to this question was that I would be anaesthetising the patient rather than looking at the ECG during induction of anaesthesia and, as I thought that it was not an appropriate question, I requested the examiner to ask me another question. Other examiners on the table supported me but the physician who asked me the question, refused to ask me any further question and told me to return in six months. I felt that this was unfair and this question was meant for Membership candidates and not for the Diploma. I never appeared again for the Diploma.

4. LONG ASSOCIATION WITH O. & G.

AFTER SIX MORE months in general surgery, I had a long association in obstetrics and gynaecology. I had honours in obstetrics and gynaecology when I qualified in Kolkata so I decided to specialise in this field. One year of general surgical experience had helped me to become a confidant doctor so I made enquiries if I could be trained in cardiac surgery but I was turned down as they were not keen on female doctors as this was a busy line.

I took up Obstetrics and Gynaecology in Morriston Hospital, Swansea, as a senior house officer. I knew the unit well as I used to cover it when I was an anaesthetist. I had exceptionally good bosses and they were incredibly good surgeons and liked by their patients. This was the busiest of jobs for me as I had no peace at night when on call because the most of the babies were born at unearthly hours.

When I started working in obstetrics, I could not imagine somebody stealing a baby from the unit but I came across a big problem when I was new to the department,. A woman delivered her baby under the care of a Consultant and the baby was found to have a heart problem which was treatable. She could not accept this so she changed the baby in the neonatal room where the babies were normally kept at night so that mothers could take some rest while the midwives looked after the babies. Following morning she discharged herself and went home with her stolen baby. This went unnoticed till another mother found her baby was becoming blue during breast feeding and guessed that there was something wrong with it. The paediatrician on duty came to see the baby and discovered what had happened. He knew there was a baby born with heart defect on the ward and this was the one. Obviously, they managed to find out what had happened and traced the mother to her house. It was sad to watch the drama unfold. Police were involved and the mother who stole the baby had to be counselled. After that, new rules appeared in the delivery suite and more work was involved. Tags were put on babies' hands and legs to identify them, and a midwife had to be present in the neonatal room. The nursing mothers could not enter the room unless the midwife was present. This became an international news story and was in all the UK newspapers as well.

I remained as a senior house officer for a couple of years before I became a registrar in the same hospital and I gained tremendous amount of surgical experience there. I appeared for the Diploma examination and I passed easily. As we were short of doctors in the hospital and there was shortage of locum doctors, it was difficult to get anyone to stand in for you. The day before the examination I had to do the night on call till six in the morning – then I took a train to London to appear for the examination at the Royal College of Obstetrics and Gynaecology.

Looking after pregnant mother is a long-drawn procedure. As soon as a diagnosis of pregnancy is made, the general practitioner referred the pregnant mother to the hospital maternity unit for assessment. Straightforward cases were booked for home births delivered by midwives. High-risk patients were booked for delivery in the hospital. There was close liaison between the hospital and the GP unit. In hospitals the majority of patients were delivered by the midwives. If there were any complications, doctors were involved.

At Registrar level there was more responsibility. I had to teach junior doctors and nurses on a regular basis. Antenatal clinics were run by doctors headed by the consultant. This clinic offered diagnostic tests for foetal abnormalities, blood was taken for various tests like anaemia, blood disorders and there was a routine urine test. Ultrasound was for confirming and dating the pregnancy; it also picked up some foetal abnormalities and was used routinely to check the growth of the baby. The ultrasound scan was normally done in the radiology department and this had been gradually taken over by the Obstetricians.

Delivery unit was the busiest place in the maternity unit. When on duty one had to keep an eye on what was going in labour unit close by. If at any time there was problem such as prolonged labour or foetal distress the doctors had to take over the care of the pregnant mother from the midwives. I carried out forceps, ventouse and Caesarean section under general anaesthesia or spinal, whatever was indicated after discussing the case with the consultant on duty. Delivering the baby in good condition was very satisfying. Instrumental deliveries can be difficult so one had to be careful. Paediatricians were also present during deliveries to resuscitate the babies and this was a great help.

During this period the doctors had to cover 'flying squad' which meant the doctors had to attend the patients at their home if there were complications during a home birth and the mother could not be transferred because she was in a critical state. Normally resuscitation was carried out before she was transferred to the maternity unit. I remember a case where I went out in flying squad with the anaesthetist and the midwife. The patient had bled so much following a normal childbirth that she was in a moribund state when we arrived. Her husband had delivered the baby as the midwife was late arriving. Trying to resuscitate the patient in the house was difficult as there were no facilities like in the hospital. The bed was low, and I had to kneel down in order to get to the patient. With great difficulty we managed to save her life. She had retained the placenta which had caused the bleeding. Under anaesthesia I removed the placenta and transfused her with two units of blood then transferred her to the maternity unit. Home births were very popular in the nineties, so careful selection was necessary for the suitability of patients going for home deliveries. Things can go wrong during labour, so Flying squad was needed.

Flying squad gradually became unpopular as resuscitation was difficult in the district. During freezing weather, it was difficult to travel to the patient due to poor road conditions. Finally the Royal College of Obstetrician & Gynaecologists took a decision of stopping this service as this was not safe for the patient.

I wanted to visit United States with my friends after passing ECFMG which is the entrance examination to work in USA. I had no intention for working in USA at that stage as I was undergoing training in the UK to become a specialist in Obstetrics and Gynaecology. I was annoyed that a visa to enter the USA was not granted as the American embassy thought that I would stay back in their country illegally. I felt America was not the place for me. People in America were big headed as their economy was stronger than other countries. Being young and not keen on politics, I was not sure about American policies.

Two years after the rejection, I was granted a visa to enter America. I visited different hospitals where my friends from India were working. Somehow, I did not like the way they were practising medicine. Hospitals were massive but mainly private, although there were Government hospitals where poor people could have treatment. Litigation was extremely high and I felt this was one way residents made money. Medicine was practised in a different way to that of the United Kingdom. The UK National Health Service was unique; everyone had access to free health care along with free medicine. Private medical facilities were only there for those who wanted to jump the queue and this sector was used by a mere handful of people.

I appeared for MRCOG examination after having adequate training while I was working as a registrar in Morriston Hospital. I failed MRCOG examination in the first attempt – I passed in theory but failed in viva. I was given a specimen by an examiner who wanted to know why a hysterectomy was performed on a patient at the age fifteen. My answer was very simple: I said a hysterectomy should not have been performed on this patient as she was only fifteen years old. The examiner did not like the answer as the examiner himself had done the hysterectomy and brought the specimen from his hospital. I am still unaware as to the reason for the hysterectomy. One cannot argue with an examiner as he is sitting on the other side of the table and thinks himself to be God!

I wrote a case report on a patient where I was assisting my boss, a fifty-three-year-old woman who was admitted with a history of swelling of her abdomen and the scan had shown ovarian cysts. At operation she was found to have ovarian tumours with her appendix involved. Histopathology confirmed the diagnosis. *Bilateral Krukenberg Tumours of the ovaries with Primary in the Appendix* was published in the *Journal of Obstetrics and Gynaecology*. This was my first publication and I was chuffed about it.

The unit was superb with experienced gynaecological surgeons. Surgical skills of the consultants were excellent. I was fortunate to work under these consultants and soon I developed their techniques in both delivering babies and gynaecological surgery. Whenever there were opportunities to learn I would be there in order to improve myself. I enjoyed my clinical work as I felt I could help patients from their illnesses. This gave me tremendous satisfaction and I must admit that the consultants also trusted me in treating their patients and they supported me. By this time I could do all different types of Gynaecological surgeries. I knew my limitations: I would ask their opinion whenever it was necessary. Most of my teaching was with this unit and I could feel that soon I would be a good reliable surgeon.

My bosses wanted me to apply for a senior registrar's post. As I had never worked in the teaching hospital and had not done any research, I had no chance of becoming a senior registrar. The main factor was that I was a foreigner so I should not climb up the ladder even if I was competent doctor. I had a few guardian angels who kept on trying for me to get a post in the University of Cardiff for further training.

Eventually I got a registrar's post at the University Hospital with a facility to do research work. I was already a well-trained doctor in O&G, so I did not have any difficulty in filling the post. But the professor did not like me as I was a foreigner. His remarks were very painful. I was told that I was trained in jungles so I needed to be observed; I replied that I was trained by UK doctors so they need not worry. I learnt nothing from that university apart from how to attend meetings and present cases. First year I carried out *Immunoassay on Amniotic fluid, Measuring Alpha Hydroxy Progesterone for the Diagnosis of Adrenal Hyperplasia in Babies*. This paper was published in the Paediatric Journal. The following year along with a consultant anaesthetist I was operating on pregnant sheep to see the effect of a respiratory stimulant in foetuses in utero. This work had to be stopped as funding was unavailable and I became quite ill with respiratory infection, a shame because this research would have helped me in my career.

I was very fortunate to have a good pair of hands with which I could perform safe and effective surgery and deliver babies vaginally or by instrumental deliveries which included Caesarean Section. I had no difficulty with the nursing staff and became popular in the delivery room. I delivered quite a few wives of dignitaries as they requested.

Videos were taken of the instrumental deliveries I had performed for teaching purposes. GP trainees were brought along with medical students to see me doing Caesarean Sections. As I was a confident surgeon, I did not have difficulty in demonstrating operations in front of the trainees. Once I was doing a Caesarean section and in the operating theatre was full of trainees, students, a GP and the Professor, I cut through the placenta which was placed anteriorly; the bleeding was profuse and spurted to the overhead lamp. There was pin-drop silence. I was quick enough to deliver the baby and managed to stop the bleeding by using clamps. It was good that this happened in front of them as they could see that such operations can be tricky. I was cool and managed the case with ease and a lot of them praised me for my skill. And yet, in spite of my capabilities, the professor hated me. Often I used to feel very sad although I did not share my sorrows with anyone locally. I used to write to my father as he was my mentor who encouraged me all the time. His words were: 'If you are good in your work you will be accepted one day. Don't give up'.

I disliked the University Hospital as there was a lot of racism. During my training period, I had to attend regular meetings where I was assessed by a team of consultants and the professor. In one of the meetings, I was told not to wear sarees (Indian outfit) and to change my passport to a British Passport – I wore sarees and kept my Indian passport till I retired as I felt these had nothing to do with my job. One of the consultants in the team told me never to use his name as a referee as he was not going to give me a reference. He also told me that he never wanted me to be in the Obstetrics and Gynaecology Department. When I joined his team, I was very cautious and carried out my work diligently. When he observed my work and my attitude, we became good friends and got on well. Later, he invited me to his house for a meal. I never used his name as a referee but in return, I helped his son in law to get a job in the department.

I found working in the University amongst the consultants and the professor, who hated foreigners, difficult. They were out to find fault all the time. Once, as I have mentioned, I was asked whether I had been trained in the jungle and was told I was wasting my time in the Department. As I had enough experience as registrar I started applying for Senior Registrar's post jobs in different parts of the country but the professor was ringing up and giving adverse references about me to other hospitals even though I never used him as my referee. I was almost given a job in the Midlands but the reference from the professor was damaging. I was told by one of the committee members in the interview that the reference from the professor was adverse and I was advised not to use his name. I was not using his name as a referee but someone from the Department was passing information to him. I had to be extremely careful all the time.

5. SENIOR REGISTRAR ROTATION

I APPLIED FOR a Senior Registrar's post in Cardiff with rotation in North Wales and Swansea. There were six candidates and I was the only coloured doctor and in my opinion, I was the best candidate on that day. However, the post was not given to anyone as there was a difference in opinion amongst the committee members. Three days later, I was rung by the committee chairperson who offered me the job. He told me that the Professor had not been keen to offer me the position.

I bought a small bungalow which was close to the main hospital as my job was non-resident. I had lovely neighbours and I did not have any difficulty in integrating with them. I became very friendly with two families and got on well with them. We still visit each other. I never had problems getting on with others as I liked socialising.

I was cautious and carried out my duties very well. I had my own operating list and clinics. As I was very experienced, I was being used as a locum consultant when other consultants were either on holidays or off sick. I had been a Senior Registrar for a long time, rotating between Cardiff University, Swansea and North Wales.

I also had a problem with a consultant from a district general hospital, who was rude and racist like the professor. He told me that he had never worked with a senior female registrar and a coloured doctor. He was making my life miserable, trying to find fault in everything I did. One day, he insulted me in front of the midwives and the medical students on the labour ward and that I could not tolerate. This was regarding usage of pain relief during the repair of an episiotomy – he implied that my knowledge was shallow as I had not been trained in the right institution. I walked off the ward round and told him there was no point in doing a ward round if I was going to be insulted. I met him in his office after he had finished his ward round and pointed out that he was insulting me in front of the medical students and the nursing staff. He agreed and replied it was because he had not worked with a coloured doctor before. I felt like saying, he had to put up with me as I could not change my colour.

It was not by choice that I worked there; I was being sent there from Cardiff on a rotation. I felt it was time for me to get out of that place as it was getting too much for me. I went straight to the Medical Director and offered my resignation, blaming the doctor who had insulted me as the reason for my resignation. The Medical Director was very kind and sympathetic and told me he would look into this matter right away and that he was not going to accept my resignation.

From the Medical Director, I went straight to my apartment and booked a call to India to speak to my father who was my mentor and adviser. Making international telephone calls was not so easy back then and I had to book through an operator; the time and day were fixed and the charges were high. I also wrote a long letter to my father updating him on my problems in the NHS. After talking to him on the phone, I cooled down as he advised me to give up the job as he found me to be very distressed and he also felt there was no need to insult a person who was coloured.

While I was resting in the apartment, the consultant came to see me and discuss his behaviour in the ward round. He admitted he would have reacted the same way as I did and now felt that it was unnecessary for him to push me so far that I wanted to resign from the job. We both agreed that I should continue with the job and he would assess me to see whether I was worthy of the position. If at any time he felt I was underperforming, I would leave.

As he was the Chairman of the British Medical Association, he was in London most of the time and I had to carry out all his work in the hospital. People can change. We eventually became very good friends and got on extremely well after the initial trouble. He even tried to create a consultant post for me at the same place but I was not keen on working there. In addition, he became a very powerful referee for me and helped me tremendously. He did not like the professor at the University, so it was good for me to have his support.

My lifestyle changed during my years working in the National Health Service. When I was a junior doctor, I had no responsibility for the patients because there were senior doctors in charge. As a junior doctor, I had to discuss the management of all admissions to our unit with my senior colleague. Gradually, I managed to take decisions to treat patients on my own.

I remember, I had to attend a criminal court as I had done a Hysterectomy and the patient had died of gas gangrene ten days later. There was no problem with the surgery, post operatively the patient made a good recovery. She was due to be discharged on the fifth day but she developed a temperature before she could leave. She was started on antibiotics. The wound had healed and investigations were carried out to find out the cause of the disease. It took a couple of days to come to a diagnosis and meanwhile she developed gas in the tissues. A diagnosis of Gas Gangrene was made; we arranged to give her Hyperbaric oxygen but she died. The source of the infection was found in the intrauterine coil device, which was still present in the uterus at the time of the operation. This was my first court appearance and I was terrified. I was trembling with fear and I could hardly speak. I was stuttering when the Judge asked me my name and my qualifications. The pathologist attending the case helped me and told the judge that I was nervous. The verdict on this case was "Accidental Death". It was an experience for me and ever since I managed to attend the courts without fear.

Working in obstetrics, decisions must be made in split seconds as there are two lives involved. If one looks into the complications arising in delivery suites, it can be seen that decisions are sometimes made too late. Somehow, I taught my juniors how this could be avoided in order to have better outcomes.

As a junior doctor, I had good holidays but this became more difficult as I climbed up the career ladder. I also had to visit India once a year to see my parents. Initially, it was not always possible as the price of the air ticket was high and I could not afford it but later this became easier.

Looking back, it is extraordinary how the times have changed. There were no malls in Cardiff, just small shops selling reasonably priced clothing. There was no such thing as designer clothes and people were happy with whatever was available. Yet, in spite of this, people dressed decently. There were few restaurants around and healthy food was sold. There were no junk food take-away so obese people were rarely seen. Since the arrival of junk food and take-away, obesity has begun to create a health hazard. Smoking was not a problem, although it was available. In later years, smoking became more fashionable and became a severe health hazard giving rise to lung cancer. With great control, smoking has been reduced but not completely eliminated. Overall, the health of the nation was good when I was a junior doctor but began to gradually decline, giving rise to ill health which has now become a burden to the National Health Service.

One thing has remained constant during all these changes – the Queen. Elizabeth II became Queen at an early age because her father, George VI, died young and she has been in power since then. The Queen has had a lot of trouble in her own family and her son, her successor, is Prince Charles who is in line to become the next King. Prince Charles was married before and had two sons but his second wife was not very popular with the people of Britain. The Queen has a dilemma about passing the throne to her son. We will have to wait and see how the Queen overcomes this problem. I must say, I like the monarchy in this country and it makes the UK stand out amongst all the other countries in the west. People round the world are keen to know about the Royal

Family and they visit the country to catch a glimpse of them. It is difficult to say what is going to happen to the monarchy in the future. There are a lot of people who are not very keen on it as huge amounts of public money are given to the royals for their upkeep. I was fortunate enough to meet Princess Diana while she was still married to Prince Charles. What a beautiful lady; I still can't understand why Prince Charles divorced her. My parents had met Queen Elizabeth II when she visited India to open the Iron and Steel Factory at Durgapur, India. That was years ago when she had just become Queen.

One of the greatest changes to the country has been the high levels of immigration. The United Kingdom has had an influx of people from all over the world, thereby increasing the population. The majority were from Asian countries. Initially, the UK needed a lot of doctors to help run the NHS as they did not have enough doctors themselves; medicine was not a popular subject amongst British graduates due to the long period of training and levels of litigation while practising, which can ruin careers. At one time, the duty hours were horrendous but that changed when Britain joined the European Union. A shift was created for covering the duty hours so doctors had time with their families. This shift system definitely reduced the training time along with no continuity of work. Nowadays, doctors are becoming consultants at a very early stage when they may not have had enough experience.

As the population increased, the lifestyle also changed. People became more impatient and hostile. Some were lazy and knew all the loopholes in the system to make money. They were mainly of a low socio-economic class, on benefits with unhealthy food habits and were obese. They seemed to suffer from a lot of medical problems as their daily alcohol intake and smoking habit worsened their condition. Also, as it was free to have treatment on the NHS, a lot of people from other countries would come to the UK for treatment. It was obvious that the NHS could not continue with this 'charity work' for other countries. Now, the patients are vetted and charged for the treatment provided and are termed as 'overseas patients'.

Funding the NHS was difficult because of the increased population. Newer techniques developed which needed new instruments which demanded more funding, as did the increase in the number of doctors and nursing staff and finally paying out huge amount for litigation was another drain on resources. Underfunding became chronic and therefore, the waiting lists for clinics and surgical treatments became long. There were discrepancies: prescriptions were free for Wales but not for England and Scotland. The NHS was a brilliant health-service provider in the UK but the public did not properly appreciate it; they took it for granted. Their attitude would change if they had to pay!

After four years I completed my training as a Senior Registrar and I started applying for a consultant's post before going to North Wales. In total I had applied for eight posts which included three in England and the rest in Wales. Somehow there were all local white male doctors, and I was the only coloured candidate amongst them, but with the most experience and I had six publications in the journals. The other candidates were also younger than me.

I was a favourite candidate for the job in Yorkshire, but I did not get it. At the end of the interview, one of the committee members briefed me that I had a bad reference from the Professor otherwise I had good references from the others and my interview was good. He advised me not to use the professor as a referee since that was a cause of me being unsuccessful. The job in Solihull and London had the similar story, the Professor again gave a bad reference. There was another coloured doctor amongst the candidates for the job and they were keen to take a female doctor, but I was not successful because of the bad reference. I was surprised to see how he could give a reference when I did not use his name nor had I worked under him either. I was not sure what I had done to him but I was aware that he was not happy for me to get a consultant post as I was a coloured person. He was well known for bullying behaviour towards the junior doctors along with a racist attitude.

Prince Charles Hospital where I worked as a Consultant in O & G.

6. CONSULTANT APPOINTMENT

I ROTATED BACK to Cardiff after working two years in North Wales where I was sent to different hospitals to work as a locum consultant. It was around this time that I suffered a huge loss at – my father passed away due to liver failure. I was devastated as I would miss my mentor. I managed to console myself as I had always known that someday this would happen and I prayed to him every night to give me strength.

I first went to Merthyr Tydfil because one of the consultants was on sick leave for some time. The place had a very bad name and the hospital was in the middle of a very troubled area. Unemployment there was the highest in the country, the coal mines had gradually closed and there were a lot of chest-related diseases. I saw many different medical conditions and a high rate of foetal abnormalities in Merthyr. This was a challenge for me as the community was very litigation-minded. One had to be very careful because the locals were very rough. Unemployment was high and the majority of people seemed to be on social benefits.

I quite liked the work as I was getting very confident and there was no senior figure to bully me there. I liked the staff in the hospital and became popular. The people were very demanding but I managed to get through to them by explaining everything I was doing and documenting this in the notes for the benefit of the patients and myself.

Single mothers were in abundance in the district and they were mainly teenagers. Slowly, we managed to set up clinics and dished out contraceptives in different forms to the women. There were a lot of unwanted pregnancies for which medical or surgical terminations needed to be carried out and the perinatal mortality was high. It was a difficult task but gradually, we managed to prevent such unnecessary operations. I must say, it was very difficult in this district as the population was very volatile and they believed in themselves rather than taking advice. Nurses and doctors played their role to convince patients of what was best for them. Single motherhood was definitely one way of acquiring a flat and financial support from the Government, support which allowed them to bring up a child independent of their parents.

On the first night my car was vandalised in the consultant's car park in front of the hospital, I rang the police and they visited the hospital three hours after I had rung them. They were not helpful at all and told me they could not do anything for me. I was very disappointed as it was a brand new car. The vandalism was not out of the ordinary. I was told that the hospital was built in the Gurnos area which had the highest number of unemployed population and the place really was rough. Often the hospital furniture was vandalised and toilet seats and toilet paper were stolen. Once, all the furniture including the television was stolen from the junior doctors' sitting room.

Then I was told that a new job was going to be advertised shortly and they asked me to apply. The health authority needed three consultants to cover its two main hospitals which included two maternity and gynaecological units. There were also three smaller units with outpatient departments. After three months the new post was advertised and I finally I got a regular post as a Consultant Obstetrician and Gynaecologist.

I was the first coloured female consultant in the UK from the Asian sub-continent.

As I had already done a locum job, I knew what was needed in this unit and did not take much time to settle down. My next job was to look for a house not too far away from the hospital. I found one which I liked but the local resident did not want a coloured person in the locality. This was conveyed to me by the lawyer but

I insisted that this was the house which I wanted and eventually I got it and remained there even as I write this autobiography.

We were three consultants in the department, and had to cover several hospitals. Running around was almost too much for us and most of the time there was no lunch break as we were travelling between hospitals. When one was on holidays, the remaining two had to cover the duties of the person who was on leave. When compared with the duties of consultants now, it was hard going. We kept our own records and managed the administrative work ourselves. This worked very well but started getting difficult once administrators were introduced. We were providing figures to the administrators and all they did was to add these up. We were led to believe that they were keeping an eye of accountability of the money that was given by the government but unfortunately it became a numbers game. How many patients were treated and how many procedures were done on the same patient, along with number of days in hospital, were recorded. Computers started being available in every department so we managed to keep a true record of our work. This was definitely needed.

I should mention about the town Merthyr Tydfil where, as fate would have it, I have spent most of my life. It is a small town with a population of 43,820 (2011 census). During the late 18th and early 19th centuries, Merthyr was a centre of the iron industry and later of the coal industry. Both of these industries required a cheap and easy means of transporting bulk materials which led to development of primitive railways or tramways. Glamorganshire canal was built to support the transport of wrought iron. By the middle of nineteenth century Merthyr had the biggest and the greatest ironworks in the world, but by the end of the 19th century a completely different manufacturing philosophy and style of business emerged with the change to steel rather than iron taking place in Midland and North England. This combined with the growth of the coal industry in South Wales. Due to economic circumstances Merthyr's iron and steel businesses moved to

Cardiff and Port Talbot and gradually coal industry closed down, bringing with it numerous medical problems mainly involving the respiratory system. Merthyr Tydfil became a deserted place as people started moving out but those who had worked for the coal industry suffered from ill health. It became a high unemployment area with much drug trafficking.

When I came to live in Merthyr, a lot of changes had started taking place. The urban environment was changing with more people coming to work and live there. A new modern hospital was built, more industries were coming in and new infrastructure was on its way. Now it's a modern town with good shopping complexes and it's a clean town with all the usual facilities.

Patients in Merthyr were very demanding and rough when I arrived. In general one would say that the area was full of medical disorders in spite of its small population. As the patients were relatively poor, litigation was high as they would look for minor problems so that they could get some money by complaining and as legal aid was readily available. This was the reason some doctors would practise defensive medicine.

First night on call as a regular consultant, I was bullied by the paediatrician on duty. He asked me to do a ward round in the evening and let him know about the patients in the labour ward. He also told me that I should ring him if there were any problems at night. I knew that he was trying to show his muscles and take the upper hand. I carried out my duty the way I had been trained and I was not going to change. Bullying goes on every job so one must nip it in the bud before it gets out of control.

I remember once when I was doing a clinic, a married woman in her mid-thirties attended and demanded termination of pregnancy. She was all dolled up and on enquiring I found out that she had already had four terminations of pregnancy and had never used any form of contraception. When I asked her why, she categorically told me that it was not my business to ask her any such question – as I was paid by the hospital to do abortions! I was stunned by her attitude and told her I did not think that I could agree to her request. She got up and told me she was going to report me to the management and slammed the door on me! She reported me to the patient services and the General Medical Council but nothing came of it. As a practitioner, I had a right to refuse abortion on moral grounds and use abortion as a method of contraception. Gradually I was getting used to the local people and this made me all the more cautious as they were, and are, very litigation-minded.

I had more bad news when I was told that my youngest brother had Liposarcoma on the thigh which was the size of a grape. The initial operation in India was not done properly; he had a second operation in the private sector in UK at the same site on his thigh but by this time the tumour had already started spreading. He was young and gradually lost his life to this dreadful disease, leaving behind a young wife and two children. This was a big loss for me and happened just when I became a regular consultant.

I was once taken to task by a patient who said I had left a drain in the wound following surgery. Normally a drain is left in the wound to prevent collection of fluid including blood at the operation site. The drain is removed when the oozing ceases. The patient brought rubber tubing to show me and told me that she had taken the tubing from the wound after she went home. I was amazed to see what she had brought to show me and very disappointed in her. Firstly, that kind of drain was never used in the hospital and, according to the notes, the drain had been removed on the third day after the operation, which was well documented. It was sad that the patient told lies against her doctor to get money. We were insured by the Medical Protection Society against litigations. These days, hospital doctors have crown indemnity but if the consultants do private work, they have to take out a private insurance.

I must say, there were grateful patients as well but there were less of them. Many a time I have helped patients in difficult situations but these patients did not even acknowledge my help.

So I got used to this culture and I felt happy when they did. I remember a patient gave birth and had a heavy blood loss following the delivery. There had been uncontrollable bleeding following low forceps delivery on a Sunday morning when I was not on call. I had an emergency call from the Delivery Unit from the anaesthetist, who wanted me to come to the delivery room as the patient's condition was critical. I rushed to attend the emergency. When I entered the delivery room I found blood all over the floor and there were two doctors including a locum consultant struggling to stop the profuse bleeding. I took control of the situation and with great difficulty we managed to stop the bleeding. The patient had gone into coagulation failure due to over transfusion of blood. A prolonged labour followed by forceps delivery had caused the uterus not to contract, giving rise to haemorrhage. Doing a hysterectomy at that stage would have been a dangerous procedure. I managed to pack the uterine cavity with some haemostatic agent and manually compressed the uterus to stop the bleeding.

Grateful patient.

Altogether the patient received thirteen units of blood, she was wide awake when all this was going on. She was very grateful to me for saving her life. She managed to report to the media how she had survived following a horrific childbirth and praised me for taking over her care. There was a small write up in the paper about how I saved her life, along with a photo of me receiving flowers from her.

Team work was very important in the unit as routine work and the emergencies admissions could be sorted out easily if the team worked together. As our unit was a semi-teaching hospital, we had medical students from University Hospital of Cardiff coming regularly for training in the unit. Consultants had to teach them and assess them to see their progress. Some students were ahead of the others; some were not so lucky. I remember there was a student who was very much involved in student politics in my unit. I hardly saw him and he did not attend my clinics and ward rounds. He came to see me at the end of the term and asked me to sign his attendance book. I refused to sign as I had not seen him. He threatened me and told me that he was going to taking it up to the college tutor in Cardiff, to which I agreed. The college tutor signed him up and I was astonished to see what was going on in medical education. The same college tutor became Professor in the unit few years later. The standard of medical education must be going down if such practices are in place, leading to a poor standard of medical care. Later I found out a lot of favouritism was taking place in the teaching hospital and there was no one to question it.

Although there were regulatory bodies, doctors serving in the panels were buddies and looked after each other so it was difficult to arrive at appropriate action. I think this process is still going on even now from what I hear. Local candidates get away with things very easily but foreign graduates always struggled. It was a shame that there were different rules for the coloured doctors when they were working side by side with the whites. I do not believe it will ever change.

I have seen a lot of changes in the NHS. Initially when I started there used to be matron and medical superintendent running the show. Consultants were responsible for the management of running their own departments. Consultants were very powerful but this was changed by Mrs Thatcher when she was the Prime Minister. Now the hospitals are full of administrators who have no idea how to run the departments. The Health Minister seems to be happy the way the work is going on. No two patients are same but this is difficult for an administrator to understand. The administrators would quite often say that beds were not used properly at weekends, meaning Saturdays and Sundays beds were under used. But on weekends only emergency work was done and the emergency team was on duty. The routine work was done on weekdays. After working days and nights, doctors needed to be off for the weekend to be with their families. This was not liked by the administrators.

7. NEW SERVICES

THERE WAS QUITE a wide variety of gynaecological patients at Merthyr, including some with cancers. Cervical cancers were at the top, followed by endometrial cancers. Ovarian malignancy was normally found in the post-menopausal patients although there were exceptions. I had few ovarian cancer patients and the youngest one was only fourteen years of age. I set up a colposcopy clinic for patients who had abnormal smears. This clinic helped in the early detection of cancer of the cervix and it also helped us to treat pre-malignant conditions. I became the cancer lead and treated cancer patients' mainly cervical and ovarian cancers. Endometrial cancer of the uterus was treated by all the consultants but if the patient needed chemo and radiotherapy, they had to go to Velindre hospital in Cardiff. This system got changed few years ago, just before I retired; now all the cancer patients get treated at the regional centre at Cardiff University. Perhaps this was a good move by the centre as such complicated cases need properly trained staff and a multidisciplinary unit.

Initially, smears were taken from the cervix and checked for abnormal cells. The patients with abnormal smears were then referred to the Colposcopy clinic for assessment. The cervix was examined with the Colposcope and swabs were taken for the HPV virus. Finally biopsy and treatment were carried out which helped in preventing cancer. The death rate from cervical cancer was high in younger women due to them often having multiple partners and early sexual intercourse. Every gynaecological unit started this service to reduce the deaths from cancer.

I convinced the management to start the colposcopy service but this was opposed by the general practitioners as they thought their workload would be increased. A lot of complaints were sent to the Chief Executive about me, so I arranged to give a series of lectures and convinced the general practitioners that there was no extra work and this service to women would pick up cases of precancerous stage of the cervix. A UK-based study found that HPV virus was present in all cases of cervical cancer patients and a vaccine was produced to increase immunity against HPV virus to prevent cancer. Nowadays this vaccine is given to the school-leaving girls with the permission of their parents.

The colposcopy clinic ran smoothly and I was very happy I could provide a good service to the local community. Every six months all the colposcopists met at different venues to discuss their cases and discussed how to take the service forward. Initial stages there were few teething problems but soon we managed to overcome these.

I was a great believer of hormone-replacement therapy. Women were taking up senior posts with great responsibility along with their house work. They were living much longer than before and their quality of life needed to be addressed. Ten years prior to their menopause, they would experience menopausal symptoms like hot flushes, lethargy, mood swings etc. At the onset of the symptoms, I felt that these women should be treated with hormones. It was interesting to see that my colleagues, mainly male, were not keen to prescribe HRT, the reason being their mothers never had it. Gradually this all changed and they too started prescribing. I remember I had to go around the surgeries to update the local general practitioners regarding hormone-replacement therapy. I took it myself and I found that it helped me tremendously. I have always believed in having a quality of life rather than living a life full of problems. The chance of developing cancer due to HRT therapy is .1% and this used to frighten a lot of women – but they did not mind being knocked down by reckless drivers on the road where the incidence is 11%. As long as these women were kept under observation either by the GP or by HRT clinics in the community, this was highly recommended.

I do not think that this was the case in India. I once chaired a meeting in India regarding the role of HRT for women and it was not at all welcomed by many, including women doctors. Gradually this has changed and it is now readily available for the benefit of stressed-out women across the sub-continent.

Starting HRT services was difficult as well. The service was discussed with the management and local colleagues: how the service would benefit the patients along with the cost implications. The aim was to improve the health of the women, so that pressure on the NHS could be avoided. I managed to get some funding from local charities and the Mayor and bought an ultrasound machine for the Obstetric unit in Aberdare as patients had to travel twelve miles for a simple procedure.

Another problem faced by women in middle age was leaking of urine while coughing, an. embarrassing situation them. They were initially too shy to let anyone know about it and were reluctant to tell their male general practitioners. Leaking urine, either by coughing or due to having an unstable bladder, was a big problem in this community as there were no urologists available at our hospital. I went to the London Hammersmith Hospital and learnt the technique of performing urodynamic procedures which showed the function of the bladder and the problems which arise and how to rectify them. It was time-consuming and I carried out the investigations myself for local patients. But it was also very satisfying as the patients were no longer sent far away for the investigation and treatment. Some GPs were unhappy with this service but I carried on until it was taken over by urologists.

I always felt there were a lot of things we were not aware of and that we did not fully understand the problems of the patients, but over-diagnosis was not good either. Over-treating a patient is not beneficial as other complications can arise. Multidisciplinary meetings and frequent, regular meetings within a department were very helpful so that opinions from others could be heard which would improve the outcome.

My waiting list was rather long and I worked hard to control it. I also did some private clinics at home. Many women would come to me as they found it easier to talk to a female gynaecologist. Some women who were insured had their operations in the Bupa Hospital in Cardiff which I carried out there. I personally did not think it was right to perform private work in the public hospital as the staff working there did not treat the private patients well. I must say that the private patients were very demanding and they would contact you for every little thing at any odd hour which was annoying.

The majority of the private patients came for hormone-replacement therapy which became very popular; middle-aged women were in busy, demanding jobs. I supported these women and kept an eye on them as HRT was new to the market and we were not sure of all the complications which might arise. Another big problem was sexual health. I used to refer these cases to another doctor in the NHS who was designated to look after such patients. These were sometimes bizarre cases and I often wondered whether the patients had anything else to do.

I was also involved in child-abuse cases and I had to go to criminal court a few times. These cases were difficult to deal with as young children were involved. I have dealt with very young children, youngest being a three-year-old, sexually abused by the step-father and the mother of the child ignored it as she did not want to lose the partner.

8. PUBLICATIONS

BEING A CONSULTANT, I had to take on a lot of responsibility. There was hardly any time for myself even though I enjoyed my work and gave the best possible care to the patients. Along with clinical work, I had to teach junior medical staff, medical students and nurses. I enjoyed teaching and took an active part in clinical meetings every week. These meetings helped us to keep up to date with the rest of the world. Whenever there was an interesting case, we managed to publish it for the benefit of others. I published quite a few papers in journals including:

    a. *Endometriosis simulating ovarian malignancy in a postmenopausal Tamoxifen-treated woman.*
    b. *Clinical performance indicators at hysterectomy*
    c. *Short-term and long-term follow-up of abdominal Sacrocolpopexy for vaginal vault prolapse: initial experience in a district general hospital.*
    d. *Kinked ureter with Unilateral Obstructive Uropathy Complicating Burch Colposuspension*
    e. *A rapid assay of 17alpha OH-progesterone in plasma, saliva and amniotic fluid using a magnetisable solid – phase antiserum.*
    f. *Bilateral Krukenberg tumours arising from an occult primary carcinoma of appendix.*

A lot of my case reports were published as well. I feel proud that, in spite of a busy job, I managed to publish so much although quite a few papers were rejected for silly reasons.

In our hospital, there was a very good library and the librarian was extremely helpful. We had regular meetings, discussing cases and various subjects that should be covered in the collection for the benefit of the doctors, students and the nurses. These were necessary for updating ourselves and we were required to keep a record of them for accreditation. Royal Colleges looked at these logbooks from time to time to see that the doctors were maintaining the standard required. Whenever there was a problem, there would be a visit by the regulatory body to check and rectify the problem.

I was member of eight societies in the country and attended regular meetings arranged by them. I presented papers and case reports at the meetings. When my senior colleague retired, I became a member of the Panel of the Medical Inspectors in Nullity Suits in Wales. I also was a lead clinician and a chair person of the Hospital Maternity Liaison Committee of the NHS Trust for few years.

9. COLLEGE TUTOR & TRAINING

I WAS COLLEGE Tutor for eight years, which involved the co-ordination and delivery of a teaching programme for all junior doctors and medical students in training. It was hectic as it was on top of the clinical work that I was doing. Many of our junior doctors managed to get post-graduate degrees from our hospital and are now holding good posts in other hospitals. Another supplementary job was to guide junior doctors to train in the most appropriate discipline for them. I can say that I have trained a lot of good doctors in gynaecological surgery. There were a lot of oversees doctors being trained and they attended the post-graduate meetings and also took an active part in presenting cases. They learnt surgical skills from the senior doctors and were kept under strict supervision when they performed any kind of surgery. The training programmes were good and covered all areas. When the UK joined the European Union, the number of doctors from the European Union increased and recruiting junior doctors from the Asian subcontinent for the hospital became more difficult. At one stage, there was a big shortage of junior doctors and nurses, so the immigration law was relaxed in order to recruit more doctors and nurses from Asia.

I liked teaching the junior doctors and the midwives. There was a lot of work involved in teaching and guiding them through their career. The junior doctors training to become gynaecologists were trained to perform operations under supervision as I have mentioned. There was a system in place to regulate how much they could do every year and their training period in this discipline was much longer than in some other disciplines. After going through various stages of training, including sub-specialisation, it was essential to pass the Membership examination of the Royal College of Obstetrics and Gynaecology. The general practitioner trainees were there to attend clinics, assess patients and assist in surgery. Their training was for six months but now that has been reduced to two months.

The Diploma examination for the trainees was not essential but it demonstrated that their theoretical knowledge was as good as their practical expertise. Before going up for the MRCOG, the examinee had to write up the cases he or she had delivered and operated on, showing their knowledge of the subject. This was a good way of training the junior doctors who wanted to pursue gynaecology. The case studies had to be submitted by assessors and only those who passed could proceed to the MRCOG examination. The examination system changed a few years ago. The trainees were not required to write up any case records. The Fellowship degree, FRCOG, was awarded to doctors who had passed the MRCOG examination if their performance and track record were good.

Teaching surgery can be tedious. I always felt that surgery was an art and one had to be gentle when handling human tissue. Some are born with good hands and they pick up surgical technics easily. Just by looking at how he or she tied a knot, one could assess a surgeon as this was the first thing to learn. The rest of the procedures were not difficult. Trying to hold the instruments in the correct manner would greatly help during operations. There is no place for clumsy surgeons. A confidant surgeon operates better. I used to assess the final year SPRs' surgical skills and correct them if necessary.

I loved operating and I taught the trainees accordingly. Those who wanted to continue in O & G but could not operate properly, I advised to change their speciality. It is better to choose a medical speciality that suits you. I enjoyed teaching and guiding the juniors and I am sure this has helped in their careers. I do not remember being rude or nasty to them because I know these things hurt. I suffered in silence; I did not want them to go through the same thing.

10. TRIBUNAL & LITIGATION

I REGULARLY PAID my General Medical Council registration fees but never had a chance to see the place until I came towards the end of my career when one of my juniors had to face the GMC for something that he had not done. This junior doctor was a registrar undergoing training and was attempting to pass his postgraduate examination. He was Asian and was unsuccessful a few times in the examination as he was not used to the UK system. He rotated to my unit from a nearby hospital. He had no problem with the language and we felt that he should have been able to pass the exam. When he was with me, he had done extremely well in his papers but then he had a call from the Royal College saying he had cheated and must have seen the question papers in advance and this was why he had done so well in the theory. He could not proceed to do his practical therefore and they failed him. He had to go to the College to explain what he had done and to show the books he had used for studying. They still insisted that he had seen question papers beforehand and he was suspended.

There was a tribunal to examine his case and the consultant, under whom he had worked before, and I, had to attend. It went on for a few days. We were not present when they bullied the junior doctor. Consultants went into the hearing, one after the other. My colleague looked very disturbed after he had been interviewed and I was surprised to see him in tears. He told me that they were nasty to him and he had not expected such behaviour. It was my turn and I was determined that I would do my best to protect this junior doctor as I found him to be very knowledgeable.

I could answer all their questions and expected them to answer mine. I wanted to know how the question papers had been leaked by the Royal College and who was responsible for this. I had gone well prepared. I felt very happy that I could fight for the junior doctor.

Our newly appointed consultant became a MRCOG examiner soon after his appointment! It was assumed that he had taken the examination papers to the hospital and the registrar had taken the papers from his room. Surely, the examination papers should have been kept in the College and not given to the examiners to take to the hospital. The consultant strongly denied bringing the papers to the hospital. I asked the President of the College what action he would take against the consultant if a junior doctor was penalised unnecessarily. Quietly, the consultant was removed to another hospital. This tribunal was quite an experience.

Years ago I had to attend another tribunal as the pathologist in charge of colposcopy was in trouble with over the diagnosis of smears and biopsies. No patient died as a result of this. I had to go to tribunal and he had to go for retraining for few months. One thing I learned from the tribunal was that no one is expected to be a hundred-percent correct; mistakes can be accepted up to twelve percent.

In my private clinic, I had local patients and some from neighbouring districts as well. Some were sent for a second opinion. Often, there would be patients sent by lawyers for litigation purposes. For instance, a young mother, who already had three babies, requested sterilisation as she did not want any more. She had a laparoscopic sterilisation operation performed but at the wrong time of her cycle. She must have ovulated prior to her surgery so she conceived. As she was not advised correctly, she needed surgery to terminate the pregnancy. Obviously, the patient was upset and had taken legal advice.

Another case wanted a termination of pregnancy and insertion of an intrauterine coil device at the same time to prevent further pregnancies. Unfortunately, the doctor terminated the pregnancy but forgot to insert the intrauterine device and forgot to mention this to the patient. The patient became pregnant as she thought that there was no need to use any other contraception device. Her dismay was understandable. A similar case, who had a sterilisation done, got admitted as an emergency because of bleeding. The urine sample she gave was positive for pregnancy test. She was treated conservatively and a scan was requested. My secretary had a telephone call saying this woman had taken the urine from a pregnant woman and was trying to sue the doctor who performed the sterilisation, showing the operation had failed and she was pregnant. A blood test showed that she was not pregnant at all. I had to tell her the truth but it did not bother her.

There was a patient who had hysterectomy but her wound would not heal. Over six months, various methods were used– resuturing done three times, appropriate antibiotics were given – but it would not heal. The husband was buying expensive gifts for her. A letter of complaint arrived from the lawyers indicating clinical negligence. Soon a nurse found her opening her wound with a razor blade in the toilet; she was caught red handed. The wound then healed within a few days. Obviously she was trying to get some compensation.

Another patient, who had been under my care for her three Caesarean births, was admitted as an emergency with acute abdominal pain in the middle of the night. She was rather obese, weighing around 120 kg. She denied missing a period. An urgent scan was performed which was inconclusive and a pregnancy test was negative. A pregnancy test can be negative early in pregnancy. As the pain was severe it was decided that a diagnostic Laparoscopy would be the best to come to a diagnosis. This was a done by an experienced locum doctor. Unfortunately, Laparoscopy was unsuccessful due to her obesity. The doctor discussed the case with the consultant on call and he advised him to open her up. Apart from adhesions there were no other abnormalities seen. I saw the patient the following day and I reassured her and advised her to have another pregnancy test a couple of days later. This test was positive and she had a termination of pregnancy in the Day Unit performed by another consultant. Few months later, she sued us for unnecessarily operating on her. As she had the correct procedure, I told our lawyer to fight the case as I felt she wanted to get some money from the hospital. A few months later we were in court and I was amazed to see that she had lost a lot of weight and was looking great. The doctor who carried out the operation was slaughtered by the lawyer and the specialist doctor on the opposition side, who blamed him for the unnecessary operation, knowing full well that the case was discussed with the on-call consultant. I requested our barrister to call me to the witness box. The opposition lawyer objected as I had not done the surgery but officially, the patient was under my care and I had the right to speak, and this was agreed by the judge. I pointed out that the lady in question was obese when she had the operation but had dieted since then. In the best of hands Laparoscopy could be unsuccessful mainly in obese patients and I pointed out that the specialist from the opposition must have had failures too. Laparotomy, the open method, was indicated to rule out ectopic pregnancy as her pain persisted. We won.

Communication between patients and doctors was very important. Often, I found that patients did not understand their operations and it was always useful to simplify the medical terms and conditions in those cases. Of course, in spite of taking great care in the management of patients, mistakes did occur. This was human error. Doctors are human beings and mistakes can happen. As long as these are not life-threatening, I feel strongly that doctors should be pardoned.

Litigation has gradually increased over the years. For some patients, blaming doctors is seen as a way of earning money. By blaming nursing staff they do not get any money. Hospitals keep a great deal of money separately for pay out for litigation. The majority of cases are settled out of court. This is a main reason why the health-care budget is short of funds. In my opinion, this needs to be looked into by officials and pay-outs should be limited so that health care is not affected. If large amounts are paid out, how are we going to provide health care? I have seen the National Health Service declining over the years and the standard of care has also been affected. This is mainly due to a lack of funding, litigation pay-outs and an increase in immigration.

11. THE NHS

THE NHS HAS changed a number of times, from matron-run hospitals to hospitals run by administrators. Consultants used to play a big part and I think they did their jobs efficiently but, somehow, this was not liked by the 'Iron Lady' who introduced administrators on high salaries to run the hospitals. Having worked in hospitals for so many years, I feel that introducing so many administrators was unnecessary. This was all to do with breaking the backbones of the consultants who were becoming too powerful, according to the politicians.

Having seen the NHS when it was considered the best in the World, now I feel it is in poor shape and has run down gradually and is at its worst stage. There is a waiting list in every department in our hospital, no matter how urgent the case. Going to see a general practitioner, one has to wait. There are more doctors doing shift duty as per European law, a fewer night duties per doctor, more paper work and less responsibility. Continuity of care of patients is not there anymore, so patients are confused as to who their carers are and no one seems to be responsible for the patient, which is like passing on the buck if things go wrong. At times I feel that I retired at the best time as I could not have tolerated such practices since I would not have been able to give my best services to mankind.

The NHS recently celebrated its 70th anniversary, on the 9th August 2018. It was launched on 5th July 1948 by the then Health Minister Aneurin Bevan, to provide healthcare that was free at the point of delivery; before it came along, people had to pay for their health care. It is the publicly funded healthcare system of the United Kingdom and since 1948 it has been funded out of general taxation, with a small amount being contributed by National Insurance payments and from fees levied in accordance with recent changes in the Immigration Act 2014. It treats millions of people a year. The service is at the point of delivery, but care is not available for every condition at zero cost. There are some circumstances in which you may have to pay, or where the treatment you want isn't available through the NHS. The cost of non-emergency dental treatment, eye tests, glasses, contact lenses and some vaccinations are not covered by the NHS. It is a huge organisation – there are roughly 1.5 million people employed by the NHS, including people from England, Scotland, Wales and Northern Ireland.

In earlier days the NHS was well organised and staff working for the organisation were well looked after. Over the years many changes have taken place and its got worse. This may be due under funding and increase in population. At present it's struggling to survive unless there is more funding.

Lately local graduates are not going into medicine and nursing in sufficient numbers. There are two reasons for this, namely long training hours and high litigation. Nowadays you find a lot of foreign-trained doctors and nurses working in the hospitals.

Services have gradually declined over the years. Waiting time to be seen is now long and so is treatment. The standard of care remains good when if patients are seen and treated early. I had to wait over eighteen months for cataract operation so I went to the private sector and had it done. A lot of people took out private health insurance because of the long waits at the hospital. I think UK should not give up on its NHS as the country thrives because of good healthcare.

I loved my job in obstetrics and gynaecology. I was busy and most of the obstetric emergencies were at night. When I was young, I had no problems working nights. As I grew older, I must say I found it difficult. Decision-making was most important in the delivery suite. The life of the baby and the mother were in our hands, so we had to be very quick and careful in decision-making. I was by nature extremely careful and that helped me with my work. Again, good training and experience help in this field of medicine. We did not have protocols when we were in post but we managed to look after the patients very well. Losing a baby or a mother in labour can be a disaster both for the family and the medical staff. The teaching and training of the junior doctors and the midwives was very important for running the maternity services. I did not have very much time for myself; the only time I could socialise was two out of three weekends.

Being in charge of the gynaecological cancer services in the hospital, I was inundated with work. My OPD and waiting list for surgery were long and I was busy most of the time trying to bring it down. Thank God I remained single otherwise I would not have been able to give that sort of service. When I look back I feel I did the right thing by staying single so I could do spend more time for the patients.

I was not only looking after patients; I had a lot of administrative work. There were no administrators when I was working and it was only few years prior to my retirement that they were appointed. I did not find them helpful and their salary was comparatively high for the work they were doing. They were attending meetings most of the time and went round collecting figures from the secretaries to see how much work was done. When computers were in place it simplified the work a lot.

12. HOLIDAYS GOING WRONG

ALTHOUGH I WAS inundated with work, I always had good holidays. I would like to mention some of holidays that went horrendously wrong. Once, I went to see my parents for two weeks in Kolkata. I had a great time and on my return, I had a very traumatic experience when I thought I would not survive. I had a window seat in the economy class and an American nun was sitting next to me. This was a Pan Am flight and it was quite an old aircraft. All of a sudden, as we were approaching Dubai, I could see a tongue of flame from one of the engines. I told the nun to pray hard as we were going to die due to the fire in the engine. She panicked and with rosary in her hand, she knelt down and started praying. The plane-off loaded fuel and started to prepare for an emergency landing. I could see a lot of fire brigades on the runway and the plane was going round in circles. By this time the flame was getting worse. An announcement told us that the plane was going to land; we were advised to take off our shoes, leave everything in the flight and go down the shoot. We had a bumpy landing then we were pushed down the shoot and landed on the ground. I got up and walked towards the bus which was not too far away.

We all managed to come out of the aircraft and there were no casualties. We were then taken to different hotels as there were many of us. Pan Am Airways did not send another flight, instead they sent an engine to replace the damaged one on the fourth day. We were happy but after a few hours we were told that a wrong engine had been sent – so we had to wait for another engine to arrive. The American passengers became hostile and started shouting at the ground staff and the ground staff started sending the passengers by other airlines to their destinations. It took six days to get from Dubai to the UK.

Another incident occurred when I was going to attend a family wedding. I went to the airport without taking my passport and I missed the flight. I went back home and managed to get another air ticket for the following day. On three occasions flight could not land at Heathrow due to bad weather so we were diverted to Amsterdam, the first time. Second time landed in Manchester and the third time in Paris.

I always had something or other going wrong whenever I travelled. I lost my suitcases four times and only twice did I manage to collect the suitcase at a later date. Once I was travelling from Middle East and there were a lot of Muslims in the flight. They were travelling for some religious festival. It was their prayer time so all of them blocked the aisle as they had to kneel down and pray. I needed to use the wash room but I was unable to go because they were blocked. I asked the stewardess to help me out but I had a mouthful of verbal abuse from them. Just imagine how fanatical they were that they would not co-operate with their fellow passengers.

I travelled a lot more after retirement. Most of the trips were guide-operated so there were no problems. I have been on seven cruises all over the world. I found cruises were very relaxing and well arranged. I felt New Zealand was the best country I visited and found it very picturesque and the people were wonderful. Amongst the cities, I would say San Francisco was the best. South America has been the last country I visited before Corona struck and I was amazed going through South America, Peru, Chile. Argentina and Brazil. Although they were laid-back people, they were very friendly and helpful. In Patagonia, a lot of Welsh people had settled and this place was like a small Welsh town and there were many people with strong Welsh accents.

13. EXPENSIVE HOBBY

I HAD A very expensive hobby. I visited the yearly motor show in UK which was held either at Earl's Court in London or in Birmingham. I was keen to see the new models which were shown in the motor show. I would look up the auto magazines to see the write-ups of the cars prior to visiting the show and every car company was trying to bring in new features to attract buyers so that cars would be sold easily. It was not that I was buying cars every year but I tended to change cars almost every two years.

Some of the car companies were very well known for their performance. I preferred the German cars for the looks and their performance. As I was keen on cars I always had two cars; one was a saloon and the other was a sports car that I used for pleasure trips. I was wasting money to have two cars but I enjoyed them and they gave me pleasure. During my working years I changed cars twenty-two times and I don't regret wasting my money. Most of the time I drove a Mercedes saloon but I changed the sports car from Honda to Mercedes and finally to Porsche. I enjoyed the Porsche very much as it had the maximum safety features and was a very powerful car. I had to have driving lessons before I took delivery of it because I had to learn about all the features. What a car! After driving it for few years, I felt I had driven one of the best cars in the world. When I bought the Porsche, I was given a pass to drive on Silverstone racing track as a token of appreciation by the garage where I bought it. I drove a 911 on the racing track with a driving instructor sitting beside me. I was going at a high speed on a simulated race track and I lost control. The car spun three times and the car took over the control and it came to a standstill. This was one of the safety features – taking over the control if the driver fails. I had few Mercedes sports cars but these were nowhere near the Porsche.

I must say that I was a fast driver as I was picked up by the speed cameras very often. It's amazing that I was only picked up when I was driving the sports cars not the saloons. I often wondered whether all the sport cars were automatically picked up by cameras. I felt I should have contested the decisions sometimes but I did not have proof apart from me looking at the speedometer, which might not have been accepted. I remember once I was coming from London around seven in the evening. On the motor way I noticed a Jaguar sport coming at the same speed. We started chasing each other, going well over the speed limit. At one stage we were doing 120 miles per hour. I noticed a police car following us, this was near Bristol. Obviously I slowed down to normal limit, but the Jaguar went past and was followed by the police car. After some distance I saw the police car had also slowed down and flagged me to stop. I was booked by the policeman for doing 90 miles per hour. I agreed and I apologised. I didn't contest it as I had actually been driving much faster than that. I asked him whether he managed to catch the driver of the Jaguar. He smiled and said, he was only driving a Ford; he could not catch up with him but he managed to get the number plate.

I accumulated quite a few points over the years due to speeding. On two occasions I nearly lost my license to drive. Once I got help from the local MP and the second time, the Medical Director of the hospital wrote on my behalf. I paid fines on numerous occasions and attended Speed Awareness classes three times. In order to experience the performance of a sports car, I had to drive fast on good roads. I looked after my cars very well. After retirement I decided to keep only one car as I have low mileage, and this car is fitted with many gadgets requiring a second battery.

14. SERVICES PROVIDED

IN OBSTETRICS, WE managed to reduce the perinatal mortality rate by safe delivery and having paediatricians available during childbirth. Normal deliveries were more common and these women were delivered by midwives; instrumental deliveries like forceps and ventouse, including Caesarean deliveries, were performed by trained doctors. Assessment of pregnant mothers during the antenatal period and the identification of high-risk patients helped us in the management of cases. There was continuity of care between the hospital, the GP practice and delivery in the local maternity unit.

When I was a junior doctor, there used to be more home births than there are today but these were gradually phased out due to a shortage of midwives and the fact that obstetric emergencies could arise at any stage of the delivery, which could be detrimental to the wellbeing of either the baby or the mother. There was another factor which was very important: women were working and were limiting their families to one or two children so they usually wanted to deliver in the maternity unit, where all the facilities were available. I found the system very satisfactory and it was accepted by all.

Just before I retired, all this began to change yet again, and more power was given to midwives with the introduction of midwifery led units. Some units were next to the consultant-led maternity units within the same premises but others were more distant. Gradually, we noticed that there was a new breed of 'radical midwives' emerging in the unit, competing with the doctors. Some of them were given 'Consultant Midwife' posts. I remember one of them came up to me, introduced herself and explained her role in the unit. There would be maternity patients under her care, she said so I thought my work load would decrease and I was very happy with that. She also told me that if I ran into any problems looking after patients, I could refer them to her! My reply to this was simple: I would retire from the NHS the day I needed to refer any of my patients to her. I felt giving too much power to midwives would be the downfall of the maternity services.

A year after her appointment, I asked her to give us a talk on her role in the NHS. She agreed straight way and spoke at one of the postgraduate meetings. She was a good speaker. She had looked after eighteen pregnant mothers during the twelve-month period. Five patients needed Caesarean sections and two had forceps deliveries so these had been transferred to the consultant unit. She seemed very happy with the service she was providing but I was shocked to see the figures. During that same year, I'd had 1,100 pregnant mothers in my care for delivery. I felt money was wasted appointing such members of staff as it was not cost effective. And we weren't just looking after pregnant mothers; there were other gynaecological patients to take care of.

Most of the time, we had emergencies at night. It was often tiring as we had to be back on duty the following morning. It became gradually worse when the UK joined the European Union. Consultant duty remained same but the juniors went on shift duty. This was the time when the continuity of care began to suffer. The 'Blame Game' started and nobody wanted to own up if there was a mishap. And when in doubt, the consultants were usually blamed for everything and their work load increased. The shift system for consultants started after I retired and more consultants were appointed as a result.

The delivery rooms were well equipped and there was a nearby operating room for Caesarean sections. Our unit was connected to the paediatric unit as this was also needed. There was a dedicated anaesthetist solely for the delivery unit, who provided epidural or spinal anaesthesia. We also had a jacuzzi in the unit which was used for pain-relief in labour but not used for delivery. There were a lot of premature births as the diet of many pregnant mothers was poor and they smoked. A lot of patients had anaemia during pregnancy due to their unhealthy diet and some were also drug addicts. Premature births occurred mainly among teenage, pregnant mothers. I think these teenagers knew that they could get a lot of assistance from the Government if they had a child.

The paediatric unit was excellent and provided a superb service. There was a special-care baby unit where they looked after the premature babies. The liaison between the two units was very effective and it worked well. We had regular meetings and kept ourselves updated with new information. The meetings provided learning opportunities for the junior doctors, students and the nursing staff. Often, there would be guest speakers from different universities. We would always discuss the management of difficult cases beforehand so that everyone was fully aware before the patient's admission. There were cases which were mismanaged but such cases were analysed in these meetings so that similar mistakes did not happen again.

The obstetric unit was an amazing place. It was unpredictable. At times the labour ward would be empty, and in few minutes it could be full of patients in different stages of labour. This unit produced one of the highest litigations in the hospital. We had insurance cover from the Medical Protection Society or Defence Union, for any legal cases and we paid for our own cover. This changed to Crown Indemnity in the mid-90s. Gradually, the UK followed the trend of the USA, where litigation was frequent. The American health-care system was mainly private with a few Government hospitals for the poor.

Over the years, litigation in obstetrics has increased. With the underfunding of the NHS and high rates of litigation, hospitals are under tremendous pressure. Midwives were not in the same category as the doctors and therefore, could not be sued. Thank goodness! The NHS was at its best while I was working there. I felt we provided the best care for the patients. Perinatal mortality and maternal mortality have gradually increased since then and the frequency of litigation is high. The Royal College had been involved in investigating the problem as it is of great concern.

In my career I had lost two mothers. One died after normal childbirth. She had an Amniotic fluid embolus after the delivery and died instantly. The diagnosis was only made after post-mortem. The second patient was sixteen years of age, had no antenatal care and was admitted at thirty-eight weeks with severe chest pain. She died within half an hour of admission. An ECG was done and by the time the full medical team arrived we lost her. Post-mortem was done and this showed a ruptured ascending aorta. This condition would have been picked up in the antenatal clinic if she had attended. Again, people suffering from this condition normally die young, but she survived till she was sixteen years of age. These were unavoidable deaths and the Royal college was notified.

In the community, there were contraception clinics where different forms of contraception were discussed and oral contraception was given out. There were other forms of contraceptives available and given to women, according to their need. These were friendly clinics, held at convenient times so women could attend. Later, hormone Replacement Therapy was included when it became popular amongst women. These clinics were run by the Community Gynaecologist. This clinic also provided facilities for unwanted pregnancies. Majority of the patients were single but there were married women also requesting abortion. A lot of them never bothered to use contraception.

Caesarean section was a common operation but not without hazards. Controlling the bleeding could be a significant problem in some cases, especially in 'Placenta Previa', a condition where the placenta is situated in the lower part of the uterus. Normally, consultants would operate on these cases, closing the uterine incision quickly in view of the excessive bleeding. I developed a technique known as 'Maulik's Manoeuvre' to control the bleeding. This was a simple technique and I regularly used it. I wrote a paper on the subject but it was not accepted by the Royal College as there were not enough cases using this technique. Bob Lynch's suture was already in use for such cases and was recommended by the College. I felt my technique was simpler and easier. I had given lectures in the local hospitals and also in India where I was invited as a speaker. I know for certain that quite a few of my colleagues were using my technique at the time.

I would now like to mention more about the gynaecological services at the Prince Charles Hospital. Gynaecological outpatient clinics were held in several hospitals but the operations were carried out in just two hospitals. All the major cases were performed in the main hospital and the secondary unit was used only for straight forward cases. Although the population was not big, gynaecological pathology was high. As I explained earlier, cancer of the cervix was high amongst younger women. Early diagnosis by colposcopy and biopsy, followed by surgical treatment, meant a better prognosis. I managed to reduce the frequency of cervical cancers although it took several years to see the results of my service. Once the diagnosis of cervical cancer had been made, I carried out the radical surgery of Wertheim's Hysterectomy, a difficult operation but as I had so much experience, I had no problems. There were only a few centres allowed to perform these operations.

It was great satisfaction that I could operate on these patients with good results. When the result was otherwise, I felt unhappy. In such circumstances, I used to analyse my performance to see what I could have done to improve the outcome. This was how I used to improve my techniques for better results next time. These radical operative techniques were difficult so very few surgeons could perform them. Junior doctors had good training in cancer surgery when they were assisting me in such cases.

The other cancer which was very tricky to treat was ovarian cancer. Early diagnosis was difficult as these patients were asymptomatic and they presented themselves to doctors at the late stage. This cancer also required radical surgery and these operations were performed by experienced surgeons, and both these conditions needed radiation and chemotherapy depending on the histopathology. Endometrial cancer, which is a uterine cancer, was the third most common cancer and had better results due to early diagnosis and treatment. One other cancer, vulval cancer, was easy to diagnose but the operation was cumbersome and difficult, and healing of the wound was slow as a wide area of skin was excised. Thank goodness this cancer was very rare. During my time as consultant, I carried out all these cancer surgeries but gradually, this service was centralised and became unavailable in the unit after my retirement.

There were regular, multidisciplinary meetings for the cancer services and statistics were kept to monitor the outcome of the treatments we provided. I must say, overall, my figures were very good and I was proud of them. We had to abide by the 'ten day rule' which meant, diagnosis to treatment had to be completed in ten days. Sometimes, I had to operate on Saturdays when I was off duty, to be within the time limit. I enjoyed operating as I found it challenging and had a good pair of hands.

As for the routine gynaecological work, we three consultants managed both the outpatient department and the operations effectively. We saw the patients ourselves and they were operated on by the same person who saw them. This was the norm in my day, but now this system has changed and there is no continuity in patient care. Wide varieties of patients were seen in the clinic. There were lot of psychological patients, worrying about silly little things, also patients with sexual problems would attend. I managed to send these patients to the sexual health clinic. Another group, lesbians, were amongst the gynaecological patients with various problems. Clinics were busy and women with a lot of pathology were seen.

Previously, all surgeries were performed by large incision so that the view of the operation site was good, meaning the operation could be done safely, but a newer technique, using a laparoscope, was developed nearer my retirement. I mastered this technique within a short period of time and offered it to patients who preferred this type of surgery. I must say, if I were to have surgery, I would have the open method as the view is better. The operation time by laparoscope took much longer than that by laparotomy.

There was a Day Surgical Unit at the hospital where minor surgeries were performed. We carefully selected patients who were medically fit for the Day Unit, to undergo minor surgical procedures and then go home the same day. In case there were complications during surgery, or the patients were drowsy after anaesthesia, they were kept in overnight for observation in the Gynaecological Ward. This unit was very friendly and caring so patients were not frightened to come in. Initially, the Colposcopy Clinic was in the Day Surgery but after a few years, it moved to a dedicated area and the Day Care Unit was used for minor, surgical procedures.

The rest of the gynaecological operations were performed in the main operating theatres. These theatres were a good size and well equipped. The nursing staffs were well trained and could assist the surgeons during operations. Some of them were so brilliant they would even keep an eye on the junior doctors. If a junior doctor was having difficulty, they would call the consultant. This was due to the experience the nurses had gained, working in the operating theatres for years. I was lucky and had experienced nurses working for me. Teamwork was important and this helped to provide excellent surgery for the patients.

Once, I was doing a laparoscopic hysterectomy and I didn't have the usual staff in the theatre. I asked for a bipolar connection for the diathermy machine and a nurse connected it to monopolar instead. As soon as I used it, I knew the connection was wrong. I stopped the operation and rectified the connection. The damage was done but I could not see any obvious problem during the operation and the damage was only picked up twenty-four hours later. I had to take the patient back to the operating theatre and sorted out the problem. There was a small area that had been burnt near the junction of the bladder and the ureter. Re-implantation of ureter in the bladder was done by an urologist. I apologised to the patient and explained what had happened. Obviously, the patient sued me as I was in charge of her care. I advised the hospital lawyer to settle the matter out of court as this our mistake. There were fewer mistakes if you did everything yourself but this was not always possible; I had to depend on others to help me provide patient care.

I had a smart junior doctor working under me who assisted me in a Caesarean section operation and asked me if he could do the next Caesarean section on his own. I thought he was brave and I explained to him this was not an easy operation and perhaps, I had made it look easy. As we were dealing with human lives, we had to be very careful and go through the proper training before we allowed juniors to perform any surgery. I was very experienced before I became a consultant. I could not get a job as I was a foreigner and had remained as a senior registrar for a good few years. Looking back, this was a blessing in disguise. I only had one litigation case against me during the whole period I worked in the NHS.

Often, we had problems with youngsters travelling around the UK. They would use the hospital as a bed-and-breakfast, coming to casualt late in the evening, complaining of abdominal pain and then being admitted for observations overnight. After a good night's rest and breakfast in the morning, they would discharge themselves and leave the hospital – their accommodation had been free. Initially, we couldn't understand what was going on as the admission rate seemed to be rather high in the late evening. The addresses of these patients showed that they were not local. We managed to control the admissions by assessing them at casualty and discharging them if they were well. The problem sorted itself out gradually.

Emergency admissions to the Gynaecological Ward were mainly due to miscarriages, abdominal pain because of twisted ovarian cysts, ectopic pregnancies and infection of the pelvic organs. Management depended on the diagnosis and the severity of the case. There was one patient who was admitted three times over a period of two months with a history of miscarriage, positive pregnancy tests and heavy bleeding. She had a dilation and curettage operation each time she was admitted and was discharged home under the care of her GP after each operation.

Sadly, she had to be readmitted for a fourth time, as an emergency with a history of profuse bleeding. I happened to be on duty that night and I had to rush to the hospital as the junior doctors were very concerned about her condition. She had already received four units of blood transfusion before I could transfer her to the operating table. I had an idea what the diagnosis was but could not confirm it as I didn't have her old notes in front of me. I discussed the condition of the patient with the husband and decided to perform a hysterectomy as I could not control the bleeding.

My diagnosis was confirmed when I opened her. This was a case of Choriocarcinoma, which was a form of cancer associated with pregnancy. A hysterectomy was performed and secondary deposits in the peritoneum were excised. She received another four units of blood as she had suffered a huge loss of blood before and during the operation. She survived the ordeal and forty-eight hours later, I transferred her to the Hammersmith Hospital for chemotherapy. As such cases were very rare, patients were only treated in two centres in the UK and Hammersmith hospital was one of them. In our postgraduate meeting we discussed this case, highlighting how it had been mismanaged. It should have been picked up when the histopathology report was available, after the dilatation and curettage operation.

One Friday afternoon when I was on call, I had an urgent call from the Casualty Department to attend a patient who had collapsed. There were no junior doctors available in the afternoon as they had gone for their Friday prayers: both of them were Muslim. I arranged everything on my own, resuscitated the patient and took her to the operating theatre as she had a ruptured ectopic pregnancy. I had to be very quick with my operation as she was critically ill. I had the nursing staff to assist me and we managed to save the patient's life. Later on, I had to tell the two doctors that when they were on duty, they could not go for prayers; somebody had to be available for emergency admissions.

A few years later, there was a similar case of ectopic pregnancy. The patient arrived at Casualty and she was in a serious condition. She happened to be a Jehovah's Witness and refused the blood transfusion. Plasma expanders were given to improve the blood pressure but this didn't work. The anaesthetist was reluctant to anaesthetise her in that condition and the relatives would not give permission for us to transfuse her and the woman died, right in front of me. I was devastated. It was difficult to treat patients who belonged to this group.

I would like to mention another Jehovah's Witness patient. This was a twelve-year-old boy who was brought into Casualty with a serious injury resulting from a car accident. At that time, I was only a senior house officer, working in anaesthesia. The boy needed blood but this was refused by the parents so I called the consultant anaesthetist to solve the problem. He cleverly took the boy to the operating theatre and transfused him with blood after taking advice from lawyers.

I used to see a lot of vaginal vault, prolapse cases in the Outpatient Clinic. This was a condition which developed a few years after a hysterectomy if the vault was not supported properly during the initial operation. The operation was known as Abdominal Sacrocolpopexy. I learnt the technique from an American gynaecologist who was performing live operations in one of the London Hospitals. It was a difficult operation but I had no problem learning the technique and soon patients were referred to me from nearby hospitals. I reviewed my patients and I had a very good success rate and published a paper in the journals. Later on, I went round teaching this surgery to the other consultants in nearby hospitals.

There were other tricky operations which I used to perform to stop the leakage of urine. Burch Colposuspension was the first procedure of its kind but it was invasive surgery so could not be offered widely. Later on, easier operations for the same condition became popular. Trans Vaginal Tape and Trans Obturator Tape were done for stress incontinence, using mesh. I never liked the TVT operation as it resulted in producing an acute angulation of the bladder neck following the surgery whereas this was not the case with the TOT operation so I preferred to do this surgery.

I was criticised for performing this operation by the Welsh Urological Society and I was not given a chance to explain my choice of surgery. Lo and behold, a few years later, lots of complications emerged with the TVT operation. The most significant was the tape cutting through the urethra meant further surgery was needed to remove it which was rather difficult because of extensive fibrosis. But the patients who had the TOT operation were fine. Hospitals had to pay out substantial amounts to patients because of the later complications but I was lucky not to have patients with such problems. The tape that was used for the operation was nothing but a synthetic material which was harsh and caused erosion and fibrosis. Using mesh for the treatment of incontinence has now been banned.

Prolapse of the genital organs was a common complaint in elderly women. This was caused by weakness of the muscles and ligaments. Sometimes, congenital weakness could give rise to the same symptoms in younger women. Normal vaginal birth was the biggest factor for the cause of the prolapse. This was why post-delivery, it was so important for mothers to do pelvic floor exercises. Although they were taught, I wonder whether the mothers carried out these exercises at home or not. In the Gynaecological Clinic, careful examination was needed to identify the problem. Mild cases would benefit from pelvic floor exercise only, but moderate to severe cases needed surgery. At times, the whole uterus would be outside the vagina, making it difficult for the patient to walk, pass urine and defecate. This higher degree of prolapse was normally found in elderly patients who were medically unfit and therefore, surgery was contraindicated. These cases were managed with pessaries which were inserted into the vagina to support the pelvic organs. This worked very well but these had to be changed every three to four months to avoid infection.

The operation for the prolapse was a repair of the pelvic floor with, or without, hysterectomy. This repair work had to be performed carefully otherwise there would be a recurrence of the condition. We provided this service in our unit and had good results. Synthetic mesh was used after I retired but the procedure produced far too many complications, so that operation was abandoned and the surgical-repair operation reinstated. Why were there so many changes in treating such cases? The answer was simple. None of the operations had a 100% success rate.

With the ageing process, the elastic tissues atrophy, giving rise to sagging of the pelvic organs. Women who were active and continued with their exercise had no problems.

Various hormones were available for treatments. For menstrual problems, the first line of treatment was hormone, or haemostatic agent, and if that failed, surgery was offered. In the private sector, doctors were performing surgery first because it was more profitable. The regulatory body rectified that easily by making sure that doctors filled in the necessary forms and maintained the rules that were laid down by regulators.

Infertility services were provided by the general gynaecologists during my working life. It was not a big issue in those days. Over the years, this sector had changed and became a big problem. Male infertility with low sperm count and anovulatory cycles in women seemed to be common factors for subfertility. There was no big demand for this service before and we managed with basic investigations and treated simple ovulation induction with a few hormonal drugs. Nowadays, there are separate centres with specially trained experts providing the service. I was not keen on this service, perhaps because I come from a country where the population is vast. I had treated a subfertility patient with ovulation induction and she had triplet pregnancy. She was keen to have three babies. She had a good antenatal period and I had to deliver her at thirty-four weeks by Caesarean Section as she started having pre-eclampsia.

I am a great believer in HRT and highly recommend it to post-menopausal women who are symptomatic. This was a replacement therapy rather than adding extra hormones and I took it for several years without any side effects. Women were frightened as they thought HRT could give rise to cancer although incidence of cancer from HRT was .01%. Gradually HRT became popular and women found it very helpful.

Once, I was operating on a cancer patient and without warning, I had a sudden onset of severe shoulder pain on the right side. I had difficulty in operating and I requested the anaesthetist to spray an analgesic around my shoulder. She got in touch with the pharmacist who refused to provide the spray and wanted me to pay for it before she would dispense it. I was stunned by her attitude; she was not bothered that I was in the middle of an operation! The anaesthetist had to get the theatre manager to sort it out. The incident was deplorable. Just think of the extra hours we gave to the health service, unpaid, without making a big issue of it. Managers handled budgets and often wasted money but when it was a genuine case as this was, they were reluctant to spend a few pounds. I had to make an official complaint as the patient was undergoing surgery when it happened. The word 'sorry' is so easy to say but it meant nothing to me at the time as the patient was under my knife and a serious mistake could have occurred.

One of my junior doctors was performing a laparoscopic sterilisation operation and I had also scrubbed as I was assessing his surgery. A registrar in anaesthesia had anaesthetised the patient. The trainee had just made an incision when the anaesthetist asked us to stop the operation and asked for the cardiac-arrest team. Nothing much needed to be done as only the blood pressure had gone down which was easily rectified. I did not feel happy continuing with the operation and abandoned the procedure. We explained what had happened to the patient when she came round, but she was making up stories, saying she could feel the pain during the operation and had heard all our conversation. I reassured her that the operation had not been performed, only a skin incision had been made and that we hardly spoke when the cardiac team was managing the case but she didn't believe me. She made a serious complaint against the anaesthetist, claiming the anaesthesia had been too light and so she felt the pain and overheard the conversation in theatre. As I was there and observed what had happened, I did not think she deserved any compensation. The anaesthetic department decided to settle out of court. I discharged her back to her GP as I thought she was a patient who would take you to task whatever you did.

One of the gynaecological registrars was performing an ovarian cystectomy by laparotomy as an emergency in the presence of the locum consultant gynaecologist. He had removed the cyst easily but used a clamp on the fallopian tube to exteriorize the ovary from the abdominal cavity. Applying a clamp on the Fallopian tube was wrong as this could have resulted in damage to the endothelium causing tubal blockage, leading to subfertility. The other Fallopian tube looked normal however. The locum consultant reported this to me as I was the lead clinician at the time. She asked me to talk to the couple as the patient was leaving the hospital in a few days' time.

I arranged a meeting with them and explained what had happened. I also told them we would take full responsibility if there was any problem in them becoming pregnant. I documented everything we had discussed in the notes but they wanted me to give them a copy in writing. I reminded them that I had not personally operated on her and I also documented our conversation. I was only speaking to them as there was a locum consultant involved in the case. The husband was a police officer and he was not happy when he left.

When I went out to my car, I saw the windscreen had been shattered. This was a brand-new, Mercedes sports car. The damage had been done with a sharp object beneath the wiper which had destroyed the whole front windscreen. I suspected that this had been done by the police officer husband so I went straight to the police station. I met the police superintendent and said I wanted him to take action against the police officer. There was a camera in the car park which had recorded what happened but they were not willing to take things further as nobody was injured in the incident. Indeed, they were reluctant to take action against this officer as he was one of their own.

The explanation given to me was that a golf ball had come from the golf course next to the car park, lodged beneath the wiper and damaged the windscreen. Nobody would believe such nonsense and I told them so. I felt that neither the Hospital nor the Police Department were sufficiently worried about the safety of foreign doctors or the cost to me for the repairs. At times, I used to feel very sad thinking: I had given my best service to the local community but I got nothing in return for it. I was not running after money but I would have appreciated being treated respectfully.

There was a case of a burst abdomen five days after malignant, ovarian cancer surgery. It happened in the middle of the night as the patient had a chronic cough. I was informed about it and I wanted to operate as soon as possible. I needed a senior anaesthetist as the patient was rather obese. The anaesthetist refused to come in and asked me to wait till the morning, despite me telling him that the whole wound had opened up and the bowel was now outside the abdomen. In spite of complaining, no action was taken against the anaesthetist as he was a local man. The patient was lucky and survived the long wait. Often, I wondered whether there were two ways of operating in the hospital, one for the local doctors and the other for the foreigners.

I must write about another interesting case. A patient was admitted to the unit as an emergency with a history of heavy bleeding. The team on duty examined her and packed the vagina with gauze and gave her blood. A diagnosis of cancer of the cervix was made so she was transferred to my unit. I took her to the operating theatre for examination the following day. As soon as I removed the gauze, there was profuse bleeding. Speculum examination revealed the bleeding was from multiple sites in the vagina but the cervix looked completely normal. There were paired, comma-shaped marks all over the vagina, all similar to each other. I inserted fifteen deep sutures to control the bleeding and I diagnosed that these marks were produced by some instrument. Obviously, I wanted to discuss this with the couple but the husband refused and stopped visiting the hospital. When I asked the patient how this had happened she answered that she had fallen from a step ladder while she was decorating. Indirectly, I told her that I did not believe her and she should stop inserting sharp objects.

Three weeks later, she was readmitted with a similar story. The findings were the same as before and she needed quite a few sutures. I counselled her and referred her to the psychiatrist. She was again, admitted after a month with the same story but the bleeding was much more severe than before. She had four units of blood. She and her mother demanded a hysterectomy this time but the husband was nowhere to be seen. In spite of telling them that a hysterectomy was not going to help her, as the bleeding was not from the uterus, they were adamant that it would. I again, re-sutured the bleeding points and transferred her to the psychiatrist.

The fourth time it happened, she went to the private sector where she had a hysterectomy. Somehow, she settled for two months after the operation and then, once again, she had another episode of heavy bleeding and was admitted under my care. I tried to send her back to the private sector but they would not have her. This time, I had a call from a woman who told me that my patient was a member of a 'hamster club' where they push a hamster inside the vagina to get pleasure! This hamster club existed only in Merthyr. I got in touch with the police and the RSPCA and they got hold of the perverts who ran the club and closed it. Finally, the woman confessed to the hamster being used by her husband. It took me a long time to find out the cause of this condition. What a waste of time as this was a self-created problem and I could have been treating genuine NHS cases who had been waiting for surgery.

Often women would come to Casualty with foreign bodies stuck in the vagina. I have removed carrot, cucumber and plastic toys. They would give a bizarre explanation saying they were not sure how this had happened. Once, there was a twenty-eight year old woman who was admitted through Casualty with a high fever. She was semi-comatose and her history was unavailable. I found a door handle stuck in the vagina which had given rise to severe infection. I had to remove this under general anaesthesia as it was badly stuck in the vagina and screwed into the cervix. She was lucky to be alive as she was very poorly when she was admitted.

I often had to make domiciliary visits to see patients in their own homes who were elderly or disabled. These women were housebound and living on their own. It was difficult to bring them to the hospital by ambulance as it was time consuming, inconvenient and expensive; it was cheaper for the doctor to visit them. I used to feel sorry for these women; they were on their own with hardly any relatives visiting them and their meals were provided by meals on wheels. Their gynaecological problems were mainly prolapse of the genital organs through weakness of the muscles and ligaments due to ageing. As they were not fit for surgery, these women were treated with pessaries to support the pelvic organs which needed to be changed every four to five months, otherwise infection would occur. They waited for me eagerly, offered me tea or coffee and were happy to have someone visiting them. I often wondered how they managed to live on their own. By living longer, their lives became lonelier; close relatives never had time to visit or ring. Sometimes, prolonging life means more miseries tend to be created with loneliness being the worst one. Too many people expect the Government to look after the elderly and no responsibility is taken by the relatives.

There was a middle-aged patient in renal failure with gynaecological problems who was referred to us as she needed pelvic-floor repair. She was having peritoneal dialysis on a regular basis and was waiting for a renal transplant. During dialysis, she used to be very uncomfortable as this used to create a bulge underneath and she had difficulty in voiding. No one wanted to operate on her because she was a high-risk patient. I offered to do the surgery under spinal anaesthesia and managed to perform it successfully. She was very grateful as the operation made her life easier during dialysis. I knew that morbidity in such cases was high but I was willing to take the risk just to make her life bearable. I also explained the pros and cons of the surgery to the patient beforehand.

I recall a seventy-three-year-old patient who had moved to the area from the Midlands to be nearer her relatives as she was suffering from cancer of the ovaries. She moved to Wales to spend her last few months in her hometown. Somehow, she landed in my clinic, requesting that I treat her ovarian cyst. The doctor in the previous hospital had not been willing to operate on her as the malignancy was very advanced and he thought she would not be able to withstand the surgery. Somehow, her sister forced her to see me for a second opinion. She held my hand, with tears rolling down her cheeks, begged me to operate on her as she could not go through abdominal paracentesis which was the draining of fluid from the abdomen every now and then. I felt sorry for the lady and I decided to operate on her malignant ovarian cyst.

I performed the surgery very successfully and managed to remove most of the diseased areas. God was on my side. I felt I offered her my best surgical skills and the patient survived the prolonged surgery. She had a good post-operative period and recovered well. She had chemotherapy and attended my follow-up clinic every year. I discharged her from my clinic after five years but she kept in touch with me. She died ten years after her surgery following a myocardial infarction. I can only say that the surgery, chemotherapy and her strong will helped her survive the disease. I received many gifts from her and she also left me some money in her will. She was a kind person and trusted my surgery. I will never forget this courageous lady, ever.

A fifteen-year-old with Morquio Syndrome, Type B, was booked under my care for delivery. This syndrome consists of numerous bony deformities. Patients with Morquio Syndrome appear normal at birth. Types A and B have similar presentations, but Type B has milder symptoms. The age of onset is usually between one and three with the condition causing progressive changes to the skeleton of the ribs and chest, sometimes leading to neurological complications such as nerve compression. Patients may also have hearing loss and clouded corneas. Intelligence is normal but physical growth slows and often stops around the age of eight. Those with the condition have bell-shaped chests, a flattening or curvature of the spine, shortened long bones and dysplasia of the hips, knees, ankles and wrists. The bones which stabilise the connection between the head and the neck can be malformed (odontoid hypoplasia). Extending the head would be fatal in these cases, making it difficult for the anaesthetist to anaesthetise them as patients. Restrictive breathing, stiffness of joints and cardiac disease were also associated with the condition.

I was not happy at all to keep the fifteen-year-old under my care as she needed a multidisciplinary team. I referred her to the tertiary centre but after attending the clinic once, she refused go back there, so I had no choice but to take her under my wing. I closely monitored her throughout the antenatal period and delivered her by Caesarean section at around thirty-five weeks. The anaesthetist was very careful not to extend the head and made a cast for her. Due to the deformity of the spine, the position of the uterus was dextro rotated, making it a difficult surgical procedure. A healthy baby was delivered and the mother made a full recovery following the surgery.

A GP referred a young patient who was twenty-four weeks pregnant for termination of pregnancy and the parents offered to pay me a large some of money. I was shocked as the viability of the foetus is officially from twenty-four weeks. I refused to see the patient and I advised that she should go through the pregnancy and have the child adopted. They thought I would accept their offer and terminate the pregnancy.

One of the GPs in the district retired from practice due to health problems. She was a good GP, her patients liked her and she was a good friend of mine. She had a gardener who also worked as a driver, especially when she went on a long-distance drive. Gradually, her health deteriorated so she depended a lot on the gardener. She also had a care worker who helped for a few hours in the house. Eventually, she had to be admitted to the hospital for investigation. Her closest friend was in touch and kept a close eye on her and her nephew came from America to look after her. She had already made a will and had given most of her savings to various charities and to her nephew. We already knew about her will as she had told us the details but we decided to check it and found out that the gardener had got hold of a lawyer and had everything changed in his favour. We were shocked so we arranged to change the will back as the nephew was there. She was slowly improving and was allowed home with follow up appointments in the outpatient department.

The evening before her discharge from hospital, her nephew spent some time with her and found her to be in a good mood, looking forward to coming home but after he left, the gardener visited her and took some food for her. We were informed that she died an hour after her meal. We were very unhappy and felt that a post mortem was needed as we were not sure about the cause of her death. Somehow, the coroner did not feel the same. The gardener inherited everything and became rich overnight. What a sad outcome. She had worked hard as a GP and at the end, she lost everything to the gardener. I was upset at the time and thought that necessary precautions should be taken wherever you live. I learnt a big lesson from this so I am now wary as I am single but I have some close relatives around to keep an eye on me. Life can be difficult anywhere in the world so one should be prepared at all times.

I would like to describe another incident in the hospital. A couple came to casualty as the woman was having abdominal pain. She was admitted to the gynaecological ward for observation. After lunch, the patients were resting before visiting hour. Quietly, the husband of this patient went round the ward, stealing the handbags of the patients. In the meantime, the wife was waiting in the corridor and she could hear some of the patients screaming for help. The duty nurses ran to the ward from their rest room to attend to the patients while this woman went into the nurses' rest room and collected all their handbags. They both ran off the ward, to the car park, where they had left their car. Police were involved but they found that the name and the address the couple had given when the woman was admitted were false, so nothing could be done. I thought the couple were very intelligent as they had planned the thefts so well and had no problems carrying out the crime.

Over the years, there were an increasing number of thefts in the country. When I first came, it was not a problem. Once, when I went into town, a woman asked me for some money because she could not feed her children. I felt sorry for her and I gave her twenty pounds for which she thanked me. She suddenly said there was an insect on my shoulder and asked if she could remove it. In seconds, she had managed to cut the gold chain on my neck, grabbed it and ran away with the children to a nearby car waiting with a driver. This happened near a bank in broad daylight with quite a few people around. How can you control these things? I can only say that such people are a menace to everyone.

I also had a break-in at my house. The intruder came in through the window in my study where I used to see private patients. Adhesive tape was applied to the glass so it would not scatter and then the glass was broken. I did hear a noise when the glass was broken but I went round the back of the house and could not see anything: the curtains were drawn and the doors were locked as the alarm was on. After I went back to sleep, the intruder crept into the study and took everything of value he found there, including cash and my laptop. It was in the morning, when I drew the curtains, that I found out what had happened. I called the police and managed to get the window blocked up and had it replaced a few days later.

My two colleagues in the unit had been appointed before me and were very well established, especially the senior one. We worked well together and covered the whole area and stood in for each other on holidays. As we were all busy, we only met at the lunchtime meetings. They provided a good service, so overall, the obstetrics and gynaecological services were excellent. The anaesthetist who worked with me was a very experienced doctor and we got on well with each other in the operating theatres. Whenever she was away, I used to miss her presence and expertise. Her sense of humour was great and she helped to run the operating theatre efficiently. I must admit that because of her, I was able to provide a good service. I should also mention that the nursing staff were marvellous in providing patient care.

As I was always so busy, I had no hobbies apart from watching the TV news late in the evening. I had to read the journals regularly to keep myself up to date and to correct the MRCOG case books which were time consuming. My exercise was in the form of avoiding the lifts in the hospital and taking the stairs to go up to the wards and the operating theatre a couple of times each day. I kept myself up-to-date also by attending meetings regularly in the hospital and, often, going to seminars arranged by the Royal College in different parts of the country. I liked West End shows and made it a point of seeing them as often as possible. As long as my parents were alive I used to visit them three or four times a year. These were short visits but meant a lot to my parents. My mother gave me the inspiration to become a doctor and my father was a mentor which gave me the strength to work in the NHS against the odds.

15. OBSERVATION OF NHS DECLINING

TOWARDS THE END of my career I could see that the training of the juniors was being shortened because the UK had joined the European Union. A shift system started, there was no continuity of work and patients were getting frustrated. As the juniors were not under any particular consultant, they did not know the patients' history very well. Consultants had to do more work than before. Gradually the duty rota of the consultants also changed to a shift system, so they had to recruit *more* consultants. I retired from the NHS at this stage.

The NHS is gradually declining. Shortages of nurses and doctors, high litigations and pay-outs. Too many administrators with high salaries in post, giving themselves pay rises with nobody to question them. NHS funding has become a real issue. The population has increased, and the newer techniques require expensive instruments and costly sophisticated imaging machines along with litigation pay-outs, making it difficult for the NHS.

Once retired, I did some locum work to tackle the waiting lists. In one area, although they had thirteen consultants, they had a big waiting list for women needing operations. The Chief Executive of the trust rang me directly requesting me to help them in getting the waiting list down. I enjoyed doing the work as there were no other responsibilities. I could see that the NHS was slowly declining and was not able to provide care as it used to. This locum work was hard going but I managed to clear the waiting list in a year. The workload of the consultants was reduced due to a shift system and I was doing more work than the regular consultant. The attitude of the patients had changed as well; they would demand rather than request. I decided not to do anymore locums as I had planned to do charity work. I have continued with my charity work but I had to cancel this work due to Covid 19 this year.

The Prince Charles Hospital, where I was based, had most of the facilities which became available over the years. I felt proud that we were comparable to other hospitals. I felt that consultants were the ones who could maintain the standards of the hospital by showing their interest in updating the unit, instead of merely blaming underfunding. Our hospital had a bad name before I joined and had the highest number of litigation actions in the country due to high unemployment in the area and a poor social class to care for with many medical problems. Initially, I was concerned about its poor reputation. As I became aware of the situation, I was very careful to give the service needed to the locals and I always fully discussed treatments with the patients and documented the discussion. I thought this was a key factor in reducing potential litigation.

16. WAWAA AWARDED TROPHY

IN WALES, A society known as WAWAA, which stands for 'Welsh Asian Women's Achievement Awards', gives awards to Asian women who have made great achievements in Wales every few years. Candidates have to be nominated and reasons given to support their nomination. A team of four Welsh judges interviews the candidates after obtaining information from the workplace. The candidate is grilled by these judges who are selected from the medical profession, the law, politics and business.

I was nominated by a colleague from a different hospital for my surgical skill. She had seen my work and was impressed by my cancer surgery. She often used to come to my operating theatre to observe. Before the interview, the judges made enquiries at the hospital and from the local gynaecologists regarding my capabilities. At the interview, they asked me mainly about my career progress and how I became a consultant as such posts were not given easily to foreigners. My answer was simple. I told them I had a good pair of hands which had helped me to progress in my career although it had taken a bit of time. According to Lord Buddha, it takes time to achieve a major goal. Local

WAWAA Trophy.

newspapers had highlighted some of my good work and printed my photo on some occasions.

There were few of us in the nominated group being interviewed and I was chosen as the Woman of the Year in the science, technology and medicine category. The award ceremony was held in the City Hall in Cardiff and when I received my trophy, I thanked the audience in the Welsh language which was greatly appreciated. I had not expected this. It was a huge surprise and I was overwhelmed. I met the judges who had interviewed me at the ceremony and they congratulated me and told me I had very good references from everywhere and I had been brilliant at the interview. I was pleased to hear this as I was very candid about my past and the abuse I had to face climbing the career ladder.

Looking back at my career now, I wonder how I managed to get through all those years. Life was tough: fighting against racial abuse in a foreign country, trying to win the hearts of the local senior doctors. None of it was easy. I was far away from my relatives and had to tackle problems on my own which was heart-breaking at times. Whenever I was upset, I used to go out and sit in the park to calm myself down as there was no body to discuss my problems with in the house. I had a lot of friends around me but I did not want to share my difficulties with them. I worked extremely hard for many years to get to the top and I was burnt out at the end. Towards the latter part of my career, my mother used to come and stay with me for a few months every other year. I used to thoroughly enjoy her company and we were like good friends and when she passed away, I felt her absence keenly. Overall, my patients liked me and often, I used to meet them in town. They would greet me and thank me for what I had done for them.

I had so much responsibility in the hospital, I often used to feel that if I ever came back to this earth, I would not become a doctor again, certainly not in a foreign country. In my day, it used to be a man's world with nurses running after male doctors. Gradual empowerment of women has changed this scene. Perhaps all our hard work, competing with men, made it easier for the next generation to fight the battle. Many women are now in senior posts, competing with men and trying to be better than them.

After my retirement, I did a lot of charity work in India. I always felt I hadn't given any service to my country where I was born and educated. It used to be a very rich country but with the invasion of different nations, India lost a great deal of its wealth and is now classed as a third-world country. Medical care facilities were divided with hospitals which provided some free health care to the poor, and private hospitals for those who could afford it. I wanted to help the needy people. The charity group I was involved with used to set up camps in remote places. Clinics were held by local doctors and I carried out the surgical procedures under regional anaesthesia. In another location, there was only a clinic and if any surgical treatment was needed, patients were referred to the nearby hospital which was eighty miles away. My last charity work in India was during 2020 before Corona pandemic.

After retirement I travelled a lot. I went on a lot of conducted tours but my favourite was cruises. Cruise ships are like mobile hotels with good food, evening shows and sightseeing trips during the day. The last cruise I had booked was in summer of 2020 but I had to cancel due to the Covid 19 pandemic.

17. PANDEMIC

I RETURNED FROM India at the end of February 2020, having heard of a viral disease in Wuhan, China, a disease with high mortality. As the disease was spreading fast, the UK Government declared a pandemic and implemented lockdown to stop the spread. Elderly people were more vulnerable because of their low immunity. People with other medical conditions were also in the high-risk group. As a senior citizen with insulin dependent diabetes, I fell into the high-risk group so lockdown was essential for me.

I wonder what the Chinese were doing with the bats. The speed at which this virus spread all over the world was almost unbelievable. India, the United States of America and Mexico were worst affected. The death rates were high and the treatment varied from country to country. Everyone was trying to find the appropriate drug to treat the condition. To start with, symptoms included fever, loss of smell, and a cough leading to breathlessness.

As the death rate gradually increased, countries decided to lock down and close their borders. Along with this, we all had to wear face masks, wash our hands frequently and keep a social distance of two metres. The death rate was high in the western world, mainly in the United Kingdom and the USA. India had the highest number of infections but the death rate was lower and the recovery rate was around 88%.

People were ignoring the rules laid down by the Government. As soon as the lockdown was relaxed, the disease started to spread again and lockdown had to be re-implemented. There was nothing else available to slow down the infection rate. It was so sad to see so many people losing their lives but nothing could be done. The

Furlough Scheme helped many businesses but again, not all could benefit from it. Many businesses closed down. Financial difficulties became a major factor. Thank God there were no food shortages. Supermarkets remained open for long hours and arranged home deliveries for people who needed it.

Of course, we were all getting fed up as the winter was approaching and the weather was changing. Just imagine, the first lockdown started in March, 2020, and the second lockdown started in mid-October. As I was almost housebound, I decided to keep myself busy by writing my biography. Whether I should have written it earlier, sooner after my retirement, I don't know; perhaps I should have. I had been burnt out from working hard for the NHS but now at last I had plenty of time to write.

Various drugs have been tried in different countries but there seems to be no consensus opinion in the management of this virus. Treatment seems to be a combination of antiviral, antimalarial, antibiotic, antipyrexial and cortisone. Some centres were treating very ill patients with a serum from previously infected patients.

The protocol in this country was to stay home and take paracetamol for a raised temperature. Advice was available from the Covid centre. If the symptoms worsened and were associated with breathing difficulties, patients had to be hospitalised as they needed positive-pressure ventilation to maintain adequate oxygen levels. London had the maximum number of patients and the hospitals could not cope with the numbers so a new Nightingale Hospital was built to accommodate them. In the meantime, the virus mutated and a new variant appeared which was more transmissible and infectious, making it difficult to control the disease. Initially, the tier system was used but nothing seemed to control it. Vaccination was only treatment that would control the disease.

Several countries tried to develop vaccines. In the UK, Oxford University started preparing a Covid vaccine which was recently approved by the regulatory bodies. America and India also produced vaccines. The rolling out of the vaccine started a month ago as I write, with those on the front line like doctors, nurses and the over eighties being vaccinated first. Before rolling out, a new variant virus appeared which was more virulent. The Government has not relaxed the third lockdown yet and aims to vaccinate everyone soon. A lot of doctors and nurses in the front line treating patients have died due to Covid 19 and the mutant virus affects any age group.

Several vaccines are now available and the Government has bought different types. Whether the vaccines will be able to tackle the mutant strains, no one knows. The infection rate, admission to hospital and death rate are high at present. Hospitals are full of critically ill patients and are on the brink of collapse. Doctors and nurses are exhausted, looking after these patients and they are also contracting the disease. I only hope the vaccine controls the variant virus too.

I felt that management of the pandemic was chaotic. Different areas had different rules and regulations. People were getting confused by the different rules and a lot of people, including a few ministers, disobeyed them. Pubs were the most infectious places as social distancing was completely ignored after having a few drinks. It was a sad time; Christmas was very quiet for everyone and families could not meet up. Although the infection rate and the death rate have been high for some time now, hopefully, by rolling out more vaccines, the Government will lower these figures. As we are in the early days of vaccination, we are not sure of its efficacy. It was decided that the second dose would be given in twelve weeks' time. I do not think that this is the right approach as I feel the booster dose should be given in three to four weeks' time. We still don't know how long the immunity will last and again, one could easily be infected after vaccination, giving rise to a milder form of Covid 19, but that would be rare.

Covid 19 has caused a lot of problems: loss of jobs, financial difficulties, loneliness, losing loved ones and other long-term health problems. Mental health problems could become a big issue in the National Health Service. I am beginning to think that our lifestyle will totally change after this pandemic. Nobody wants to remember 2020. Many people lost their lives and the country will be in recession as everything has come to a standstill. But we may be winning at last with the mass vaccination programme. Let's hope that better days will be here soon with no more suffering.

Having worked as a consultant in the NHS on the front line, I am now on the receiving end and see the problems from the other side. When you need something done, it can be difficult. There is a long waiting-time to see a GP. Initially, GPs try to treat the patient before referring them to a specialist then there is a long wait to get an appointment with the specialist in hospital. With health insurance cover, you can go through the private sector, of course. As I am a diabetic patient, my insurance cover would be very expensive and again, doctors don't like diabetics to have private treatment. I am lucky that for my diabetes, I go to see a consultant physician in the hospital twice a year. I must say, my physician has been extremely good and has kept a careful eye on me. I hope he will continue to look after me.

With the viral pandemic, routine work had a come to halt resulting in long waiting times for other conditions. Cancer patients had not been operated on at the right time. They were not followed up on time either. Routine operating waiting time for any operation has gone up and many patients have to wait longer than a year to be operated on. Let's hope that with mass vaccination, we can say goodbye to Covid 19 and get on the routine work.

18. FINALLY

EVERY GREAT JOURNEY comes with difficult times, but one must face these to reach the goal. As a newly qualified doctor, I travelled 7,000 miles from Kolkata to Wales to gain knowledge and experience and to obtain post-graduate qualifications in a foreign country. `Tapati`, my first name means 'Daughter of the Sun', a goddess who had similar energy, patience, and determination to rise to the top. All the adversity I have had in my life, all my troubles and obstacles, have only strengthened me and helped me to achieve my goal. All along, my guarding angels have guided me and helped me in difficult times. One should remember that success is a key to happiness and positivity. Being the first woman from the Asian subcontinent to get a consultant post in UK was a great success and my journey reflects wider cultural issues around discrimination. Being in close touch with people and helping them out from their sufferings made me feel great and I feel that I have done what I always wanted to do. I travelled such a distance to fulfil my dreams and now have forgotten many obstacles from the past. I still have the energy to do more charity work for Kolkata – I cannot forget my motherland as I was born and educated, where I achieved the strength that I needed for my existence.

I hope that the National Health Service continues, for the benefit of the people of Britain. It is unique to this country. Overall, I have liked working here and gained a lot of knowledge and experience. I gave my best service to the NHS for the benefit of women. Merthyr Tydfil had a good gynaecological service and I feel proud that I could contribute to it along with my colleagues. After all, the NHS was the dream of Aneurin Bevan, a Welsh

Labour Party Politician who was Minister of Health in Clement Attlee's Labour Government.

I have fond memories of Merthyr. Over the years, this place has changed so much from the coal mining town that it used to be. Although there are no big industries any longer, it is a town with plenty of big-name shops. A lot of people come here for shopping as there are plenty of free car parking areas. I will always remember this place as I lived here for thirty years after becoming a consultant. It is my second home and I love it.

Writing this autobiography was an adventure. The journey from Kolkata to Wales had been enjoyable and well worth taking. I have described the hardships that I went through, fighting the battle alone in a country far away from my own. I know that it is easy to stand in the crowd but it took courage to stand alone. I achieved what I came here for although it took a long time.

When I look back, I am glad that I never gave up but always carried on with my hard work and forgot those who hurt me. Perhaps I inherited my strength from my ancestors. I always felt that when I was going through hard times, that they were not going to be there forever; good times would certainly follow. I like this quote from Buddha 'Never regret a day in your life, good days give happiness, bad days give experience, worst days give lessons and best days give memories'. My journey was long and tiring, but I managed to cope because, at the end, achieved what I had dreamt of.

Now I am happy enjoying the sunrise every morning.

Medicine is a Noble profession, do not destroy it.

Printed in Great Britain
by Amazon